CW01497354

I'm Free!

I'm Free!

The Life and Times of John Inman

David Clayton

First published 2024

The History Press
97 St George's Place, Cheltenham,
Gloucestershire, GL50 3QB
www.thehistorypress.co.uk

British Library Cataloguing in Publication Data.
A catalogue record for this book is available from the British Library.

ISBN 978 1 80399 285 3

Typesetting and origination by The History Press
Printed and bound in Great Britain by TJ Books Limited, Padstow, Cornwall

MIX
Paper | Supporting
responsible forestry
FSC® C013056

Trees for Life

This book is dedicated to my beautiful wife Sarah and
our incredible children, Harry, Jaime and Chrissie.
As the great John Candy once said, 'Love is not a big enough word.'

Contents

Acknowledgements

When you begin any biography, deciding where to start can be a bit of an issue. The usual process, having done your initial background research and created a timeline, is to start contacting agents and trying to trace friends and family – many of whom have no online presence – plus people who have drifted out of the public eye or retired.

I was very lucky writing John Inman's book in that I ended up with some incredible help from some very special people and, as I went along, the insights provided by one of John's oldest friends, Peter Richards, became central to everything I did. To get to Peter, I had the wonderful assistance of Doremy Vernon, who is one of the few remaining cast members from *Are You Being Served?* Doremy helped me open so many doors and her wonderful encouragement and determination to bring me incredible contacts, phone numbers, stories and to share her opinion was above and beyond. I couldn't have written this book without her.

Later, I was delighted to receive a Facetime call from the wonderful Miriam Margolyes and, in turn, she introduced me to an old friend of John's, Christine Ozanne, who I would later christen 'Miss Marple'. Christine gave up her time to interview Peter Richards on my behalf and to field endless questions, and I honestly think this book wouldn't have been half as detailed without her wonderful assistance. I am deeply indebted.

Paul Mead was another excellent source of early information, but this is just the tip of the iceberg because writing *I'm Free* has been a real pleasure and it has allowed me to speak with some amazing people. People like Melanie Stace, a former co-host on *The Generation Game*, who couldn't do enough to help me, and Susan Belbin, former production manager to David Croft, who gave me a rare interview about her years working with John on the show. Fantastic people with warm, vivid memories of John.

I could fill a chapter thanking everyone – the superb BAFTA-winning actor Jason Watkins gave me time during his hectic schedule to recall playing John Inman in the 2016 tribute show of *Are You Being Served?* – but the tendrils of this biography literally stretch around the globe, with Australia and the United States featuring prominently.

Tony Hare, one of the BBC's top comedy scriptwriters, also shared his wonderful memories of working with John

Actress Sherrie Hewson, star of *Coronation Street, Benidorm, Loose Women*, another star of the 2016 remake of *Are You Being Served?*, was only too happy to share her memories of John.

Mr Spooner himself, Mike Berry was my very first interview and along the way I also got to speak with John Lloyd, Jeffrey Holland, Barry Creyton, Melvyn Hayes, Bobby Crush, Su Pollard, Jimmy Cricket, Les Dennis, Joanna Lumley, Brian Blessed, Shane Bourne, Gary Wilmot, Joanne Heywood, Rula Lenska, Bill Young, Alex Needham, Niall Gavin, Liam Rudden, Fay Hillier, Peter Symonds, Richard Curtis, Sally Grace, esteemed Australian TV star Christine Amor, Sallyann Webster and many more …

Also, there are the words of the wonderful Mark Gatiss, *Times* journalist Matthew Parris, plus the help of countless agents – many very helpful, a few not so much! – and the valuable contributions of Alistair Smith of *The Stage*, Helen Nicholas at the *Blackpool Gazette*, Paul Middleton, Graham Robson, as well as the fantastic resources and info supplied on pantoarchive.com and theatricalia.com which proved invaluable during my research.

Thanks to John's friends for providing many of the illustrations. Every attempt was made to track down credits, but any oversights will be corrected in future editions.

Of course, there are people who are 'invisible' in many ways, but equally important. Mark Beynon, my long-suffering commissioning editor at The History Press, was as patient as always and is continually supportive of my ideas as deadlines sailed into the rearview mirror. This is the fourth biography I have done with Mark, and I also think it is the best. But then I would say that.

Last but not least, to my wife Sarah and our three kids, Harry, Jaime and Chrissie – the 'kids' all being bigger and smarter than I am now – thank you for allowing me to immerse myself in the 'spare time' I had outside my day job as a journalist.

Again, thank you so much to everyone for sharing their many memories of John Inman. He was a much-loved man, that's for sure.

Introduction

I don't believe in coincidences and think everything that happens has purpose. The first ever episode of *Are You Being Served?* was screened on my birthday on 8 September 1972, and John Inman was buried on my wedding anniversary on 23 March 2007.

That may seem insignificant to some people, but not to me. Some things just feel written in the stars, don't they?

I must admit, I was surprised nobody had written a biography of John Inman when I first floated the idea to my editor.

I was a kid when *Are You Being Served?* was at its height and I always remember laughing and enjoying a show that had a wonderful cast with sharp, witty scripts.

Mr Humphries was hilarious, and even at a very tender age, I knew his character was somehow different. While I might not have understood completely that he was almost certainly gay, he introduced a campness into the living rooms of millions of people and, along with Larry Grayson, proved to be incredibly popular to young and old alike.

It's easy to forget what a huge star he became in Britain, Australia and the United States. He was also loved in the Netherlands, Canada and many other countries that screened *Are You Being Served?*

But I was intrigued to find out how this fame came about – was it an overnight success or did he have a long body of work that perhaps not many people knew about that led into it? Plus, what happened to him after the show finally ended its thirteen-year run?

What I discovered in the pages that follow, told through the eyes of close friends and colleagues, is that John Inman was greatly admired and, though he kept his private life private, once he stepped on to a stage, in front of a camera or appeared as a dame in any number of pantos, he was the consummate professional and a wonderful entertainer, hellbent on sending people home happy.

You'll learn all about that as you go along, and at the end of the book, I speak to a number of journalists, commentators and actors to try to find out whether John Inman forwarded the cause for gay people or did their fight for equality more harm than good. I think it is a fascinating end to the journey, and I thank *The Times* and *The Guardian* for permission to use a couple of very powerful articles that appeared after John's death.

I hope you enjoy John Inman's life story as much as I did writing it.

David Clayton
Cheshire, January 2024

1

Born to Perform

Some people, they say, are born to perform.

They have an innate desire to entertain others, stand in the spot-light and milk the applause for all it is worth. It's in their blood and seems to be pre-programmed into their DNA and, no matter what, they will make their dreams become reality by hook or by crook.

Their path to fame and (sometimes) fortune might be full of chal-lenges, obstacles and hurdles, but they find a way, eventually, using a mixture of talent, the odd break here and there, a few white lies and, most of all, because they are driven to find that stage to perform on and that spotlight to stand in.

All of the above is true of Frederick John Inman, who was born on 28 June 1935, at 18 Garden Street, Preston, in Lancashire. It was a modest terraced family home, just a stone's throw away from the nearby Avenham Park and the River Ribble.

He was Frederick Inman and Mary Rawcliffe's first child – they would have another son, Geoffrey, a few years later – and he was born into a household of moderate income and occasional domestic abuse. In later years, John would say that his father was 'a drinking man who used to knock my mother about' – though understand-ably, he would never say much more than that.

His parents were both hairdressers – Frederick was a master hair-dresser, no less. John's first few years in Preston were sometimes upsetting as his father took his own frustrations out every now and then on Mary, leaving their son to escape into his own world, one filled with sparkles and wonder.

The first inklings that the Inmans' first-born might have stars in his eyes came when he began to hold mini concerts in the back garden for friends and family, which would always be a mixture of song and dance. The applause at the end was all he needed to fuel his passion and by the age of 5, he had a number of characters that he had developed, including his showstopper, 'Bill'.

'He was always singing and dancing and inventing characters,' recalled his mother in 1976. 'One character was called Bill and he'd use his grandfather's walking cane, go behind the curtain and the door and make his entrance. He'd say, "Bill's here!" and then start to dance.'

John began his education at Cambridge House School, and it wasn't long before he'd found a new audience to entertain, invent-ing sketches with his friends as the Second World War progressed. Preston would escape largely unscathed from the Luftwaffe air raids, though the German bombers would pass high over the town on their way to military targets in Barrow-in-Furness some 70 miles north.

John and pal Peter Diamond would perform shows in Peter's garage at 214 Brockholes View, creating their own theatre among the various bric-a-brac that was stored there, including their own pro-duction of *Cinderella*. Years later, John would regale the story and add, 'And no – I wasn't Cinderella!'

Their first 'professional' show was at the New Victoria pub on Church Street in town, and it was perhaps here more than anywhere before that convinced John that his future lay in showbusiness.

He idolised movie star, dancer and entertainer Betty Grable and he had an innate talent to design and create glitzy dresses and costumes for his own performances, often inspired by Grable's Hollywood glamour. His mother encouraged his artistic leanings, even paying for him to take elocution lessons at a local church to give him a chance of perhaps winning less colloquial roles in the future – something few northern actors and entertainers ever quite seemed to shake off in their bid for national acclaim.

Like any family in Britain at the time, the Inmans suffered during the war with restrictions on movement and rationing causing them to reassess their lives and ambitions to give their sons the upbringing they wanted. So when the conflict ended in September 1945, Frederick and Mary decided they wanted something different. Their marriage had not been without its problems, but Mary was committed to her husband in spite of the beatings she would occasionally suffer.

The country was slowly recovering from almost seven years of conflict and continued shelling from the Nazis and there was a collective hunger and thirst to move forward and enjoy life again. Fortunately, the Inmans didn't have to look too far to find everything they wanted and more, and for 13-year-old John Inman, it was manna from heaven.

The family moved 17 miles west to Blackpool – a place they'd always loved and frequently visited – and bought a boarding house at 55 Banks Street in the seaside town. Conveniently located just a few hundred yards from Blackpool Talbot Road Railway Station, the Irish Sea was visible at the west end of Banks Street and with the promenade, beaches that stretched for miles and trams making for a bustling, vibrant spectacle.

But what thrilled and delighted the impressionable John more than anything was the fact that Blackpool was the entertainment capital of Britain, with its many theatres and concert halls attracting all the top acts of the era. And he would see them all, saving his pocket money to go and watch some of the biggest acts in vaudeville, soaking it all up with vociferous enthusiasm, none more so than his comedy idol Frank Randle, who was a huge star in the north of England and the man who, more than any other, inspired the teenager to follow his showbusiness dreams.

During an interview for US TV, John would later recall those heady days on the Fylde coast:

All the stars came to Blackpool and Frank Randle was the biggest draw of them all. People would queue for hours to see him. I'd go and see him for one and six in the stalls and he'd come on stage with his boots on the wrong feet and hold the audience in the palm of his hand for as long as he liked – and he succeeded by just being himself.

I saw things like Happidrome with Harry Korris, Cecil Frederick and Robbie Vincent and had been an avid listener to the show on the radio. They were a great trio and very popular who played to packed halls. They were also great favourites of mine.

A few years later there was a show on the North Pier called Lawrence Rides on With the Show featuring Albert Modley, and I went to see him do his act and he was another of my idols.

These were magical, intoxicating days for John.

Now attending Claremont School in Blackpool, he became involved in the theatrical productions and enjoyed creating props, sound effects and other aspects of backstage management. Commenting that one particular sound effect of a character falling in a river sounded more like a 'sugar lump dropping in a tea cup', John and friend Tommy DeVere found an old bathtub, filled it to the brim and then dropped a hefty boulder in as they recorded the splash, which also drenched the pair in the process.

'Now that's a body falling in water,' commented John, before turning to his pal and claiming, 'but you've ruined my make-up!'

His penchant for performing and his understanding of theatre meant that when any auditions were advertised – and he scoured for them in the local papers continually – he was well placed to go along and try his luck.

John Inman was no ordinary 13-year-old, and his effeminate voice, openly camp behaviour and light on his feet gait could easily have led to him being bullied by his contemporaries, but his ability to make others laugh was also his best protection and he was a well-liked schoolmate.

He had not been resident in Blackpool for more than a few months when he won a part in a play called *Frieda* at the South Pier Pavilion, playing the lead's son and immediately catching the eye with a mature and comedic performance beyond his years. The Jack Rose Repertory Company paid him the not insubstantial sum of £5 per week – the equivalent of £227 in 2024 – to appear in the play and the management were suitably impressed enough to give him part-time work as a general dogsbody, making tea, cleaning up, helping with props and sets after the run in the show ended, and he loved every minute of what was, in effect, his apprenticeship in showbusiness.

John would fill in roles here and there and be continually in and around the various productions, plays and shows, meeting actors, bringing them cups of tea and chatting to them about their craft and learning all the time. He could also watch their performances for free when he wasn't involved and was also now earning enough to pay admission for whatever entertainer he fancied seeing.

Blackpool was a thriving, energetic place to live with hundreds of thousands of tourists packing out the town's theatres, concert halls, hotels, boarding houses and bed and breakfasts during the spring and summer months, with the famous Blackpool Illuminations extending the holiday season well into the autumn.

At Claremont School, aged 14, he took on his first starring role in the production of *Aladdin*, playing the classic pantomime villain Widow Twankey in a costume designed by his own fair hands. His comical performance stole the show and he helped create a 'boy mangle' that he would turn and 'flatten' out schoolmates as they were sandwiched between two rollers, to the delight of the gathered parents, teachers and fellow pupils. It was his first public display as a pantomime dame and the reaction he received would lead to a love affair with panto that would last all his life.

Within a year, John's joyous time at Claremont had ended and, aged 15, he left school to seek his fortune. It was 1950 and a whole new set of opportunities lay before him, but first he had to earn his keep.

Given his artistic talents and dressmaking skills, it was perhaps no surprise that he was taken on as a trainee window dresser at Fox's Department Store on Church Street in the town centre, and there he would be based in the gents' outfitters department. His boss Jack Holden recalled, 'He was a jolly good assistant, eager to learn, easy to teach – I was sorry in many ways that I eventually persuaded him to leave and go to London and I'm pleased to say that, having applied for the job I'd suggested, he got it.'

Of that time, John remembered, in an interview from 1976:

I never used to do any work! Jack did it all while I made props in the fitting room! He used to come in and say, 'There's a customer here, John,' and I'd look up and he'd just add 'Oh, I'll see to it you just get on with whatever you're making.'

John still had time to put on a performance of *Mother Goose* at the local church and brother Geoff recalled how he later felt the sharp edge of his brother's tongue. He said:

John made the costume by himself, and I had to go into it with a little peephole at the front and when I came on stage his face looked a bit naughty because there was smoke coming out of the gills, which was me having a crafty drag on a Park Drive!

He stayed at Fox's until he was 18, but his boss felt John was destined for bigger and better things. He had outgrown Blackpool somewhat and Jack Holden told his protégé that he needed to spread his wings and head for the bright lights of London.

When a position at the prestigious Austin Reed flagship store in Regent Street in London was advertised, Holden encouraged John to apply – and, as stated previously, he was successful in his application. It meant uprooting from the north for the first time in his life and at

18, he'd be standing on his own feet without his family around him in a new and much bigger city. He found a £3 per week bedsit and was soon sewing costumes for the many nearby theatres to augment his modest income.

Typically, he took it all in his stride and was soon a popular member of the gents' outfitters he now worked for. And, much like the future Mr Humphries he would achieve worldwide fame with, he never missed an opportunity to have fun, managing to supress a smile as he stood in the window on one occasion holding a sign that said, 'Available in other colours'.

One former colleague, Eddie Whitehouse, recalled how quickly John made an impression for both his professionalism and the ability to make anyone and everyone laugh.

'Each Friday, we'd join all the other members of the department to discuss the week's work,' he said:

John was always late for our Friday meetings – always. Anyone else would have got into trouble but not John – he used to breeze into the office with the boss with everyone glaring at him for being late, but he soon had everyone in stitches because he'd say, 'What's up? Have I missed the start of a big film?'

His boss, Ron Dyer concurred, adding: 'It was impossible to lose my temper with John – he was so funny – but he was also very good at his job. But I knew he wouldn't stay with us long because he told us constantly of his real ambition, which was to go on the stage.'

Indeed, just two years later, the 21-year-old John Inman decided it was now or never and in 1956 he handed in his notice, which the company accepted reluctantly. He'd decided that he had to get a foot on the theatrical ladder somehow and four years of working in a men's department had not curtailed his dreams of being in show-business – if anything, it had fed his hunger even more. Time and tide waited for no man and if the theatre wasn't going to come to him, he had to find a way to go to it and make things happen, one way or another.

2

Winging It

During his time at Austin Reed, John had become friends with BBC newsreader Kenneth Kendall, who worked alongside him for a short time. Kendall, eleven years older than John, was a free-lance newsreader for the BBC and also an actor who was part of a repertory company based in Crewe. Kendall enjoyed John's company, and he could also see he had a talent that needed a break of some kind, so he offered him a job as part of the company – which John readily accepted. It meant returning north again to live in the Cheshire town, best known for its vast railway junction, but it also meant he was just a relatively short train ride back to Blackpool to see his parents whenever he wanted to.

In 1986, on Mike Craig's *It's a Funny Old Business* show on Radio 2, John recalled:

A mate of mine [Kendall] was taking a Rep company to Crewe, and they didn't have a scenic artist, so I said, 'Well I'm a scenic artist so I'll come and paint the sets.' I wasn't, but I had done some set painting, but it wasn't exactly my job stamp. So I went along and did that for ten weeks in Crewe.

On the second or third week, they were doing an Agatha Christie play – *The Spider's Web* – and they didn't have enough people. So not only did the stage manager get roped in to play a part, so did everyone else, including me – the scenic artist – and I played the part of a 65-year-old Justice of the Peace called Hugo Birch and I got wonderful notices for it!

Being part of the company meant he was immersing himself in the acting world, and he was soon regularly performing in weekly plays at Crewe's Lyceum Theatre with a group of seven or eight actors. The roles would be varied, but it would enable him to get the one thing he needed most to progress his fledgling career – an Equity card – something no professional actor could find work without.

He spent a few months in Crewe before returning to Blackpool, where his brother Geoff helped him get a job working with his employers – at a gents' outfitters! It felt as if things had come full circle and he was back working in menswear in Blackpool again, but far from feeling sorry for himself or having his tail between his legs, he knew it was just a temporary bump in the road for his acting career and he continued to perform whenever the chance came, working on a casual basis with his brother and making costumes for the theatres of Blackpool when he wasn't on stage.

'That's how it started,' said John on his time in Crewe:

and it sort of snowballed from there. I decided I didn't really like being a scenic artist because it's a dirty job, so I became a stage manager. And then I started to go from rep company to rep company with chunks of labour exchange in-between. I'd always been a bit nifty with a needle, so I'd make costumes when I wasn't acting.

But John was always on the lookout for new opportunities, and it wasn't long before he found a job advert he liked the look of. The Royal Theatre in Chester was looking for a stage manager and his application resulted in an interview with theatre boss Arthur Lane.

Though John had performed all the roles of a stage manager over the past few years, he'd never actually been employed as one, not that he was going to let that stop him. Speaking during a TV interview in 1976, Lane — who had played many small roles himself in films — recalled that job interview with great clarity: 'I met him, and John said, "I'm the finest stage manager in the business" — and I believed him!'

John was back fully immersed in the showbusiness world again and would continue to fill in acting roles here and there as the 1950s wore on. He was making a living being in and around the theatre, without appearing in the spotlight, but that was as close as he could get without anything stellar on his CV. Yet.

This continued into the new decade and, now aged 26, John must have had grave doubts that he would ever progress from stage management to regular acting roles. But finally, the opportunity he had waited for presented itself — and it came in his home town.

Arthur Lane recalled during John's 1976 *This Is Your Life* TV broadcast:

> John was still my stage manager and we'd taken a production to the Grand Theatre in Blackpool At 4.30 p.m. on the opening night, the leading man came up to me pointing to his throat, but I couldn't hear a word he was saying.
>
> I said, 'Are you telling me you've lost your voice?' and he handed me a doctor's certificate saying he had acute laryngitis. I had to think on my feet, so I said, 'John, take a script — go in the dressing room, you're on tonight playing the lead.'
>
> He said, 'What about my uniform?' I told him to put on the one we had, and he said, 'But this was made for a man who is six-foot four!'
>
> I said, 'John, don't make this difficult! The curtain's up in an hour's time.' Before we began, I went out front and explained to the audience what had happened and they gave John a standing ovation when he came on — he had the script in his hand throughout and if he looked at it twice during the show, that was as much as he did.

John had proved beyond doubt that he could hold his own in a production and the fact he had done everything at the drop of a hat was testament to his professionalism, versatility and ability – not to mention confidence.

Arthur Lane was delighted, and John was handed various roles as he toured with Lane's company for several months. Here he met his first boyfriend of note in Kenneth Hendel. John had never made being gay anybody else's business and it was still a time when homosexuality was frowned upon, but his relationship with Hendel was not a secret in the theatre world. The pair were discreet but were clearly 'an item'.

Actress Christine Ozanne was part of the Chester rep company and she recalls:

I first met John at the Royalty Theatre in 1962, which closed for good in 1966. John was the stage manager at the time and filling in acting gaps here and there when an opportunity arose.

Arthur Lane was the central character in most of the productions there and he was terrible! He was a rogue and vagabond! We did a tour in 1962 – maybe six or seven dates around the country in a terrible play called *Done in Oils* about an interior decorator and John was one of a couple of decorators.

He got all the laughs with his flat cap up a ladder and he was so funny. John made all his own costumes – absolutely everything. I remember seeing him once make a wig out of wood shavings as he planed a piece of wood and took these curly thin strips of wood and created a wig – he was a genius.

It was around this time that John also met and became close friends with Barry Howard, with the pair instantly clicking with their roguish sense of humour and love of dressing up as dames. It would be a friendship that lasted many years and would become particularly profitable when they began playing the Ugly Sisters in panto productions of *Cinderella* in years to come.

'When John sang in panto with Barry, it was a bit like Flanagan and Allen – one kept the tune while the other more or less spoke the words,' recalled Ozanne.

John had outgrown rep and was ready for bigger and better things. His star was slowly ascending and the opportunities for better work were more frequent – one offer in particular, working for two renowned theatre impresarios, would pay off handsomely. In a 1986 TV interview, he recalled:

> I actually got a very good job in 1962 working for George and Alfred Black and got paid an enormous amount of money – £25 per week, which was a fortune at the time.
>
> I was in a play called *What a Racket* for the summer season at the Arcadia in Scarborough and Albert Modley played my father – it was his show – and he was marvellous to me.
>
> I learned a valuable lesson in that, too. Albert was cleaning my shoes because my character was going to be a teenage pop star and his dad – Albert – was out of work. That was the whole premise of the story, and we had this scene when he said, 'You can't go on like this – what are you going to be in a couple of years' time?' – and I said, '18 dad' and he'd clip me around the ear with this brush.
>
> But instinctively, I was standing about two feet upstage, which meant that Albert had to turn his neck around to look at me and say the line. Alfred Black was watching the rehearsals and he said, 'John, come over here for a moment', which I did. He then said: 'We're paying Mr Modley a lot of money – a lot more than we're paying you – and we don't want to see the back of his neck … we want to see his face, so if you can come down stage a little bit, that would be perfect.'
>
> And that's another lesson I never forgot. After that, George and Alfred used to look after me and I was given a part in a summer farce with Sid James in *Wedding Fever* and by also playing outrageous characters in various shows.
>
> I worked very well with Sid, and I remember in one scene, I did my first ad lib and thought I was going to get in trouble for it. My character was sat at a table and the woman I was visiting offered me a cup of tea. She gave me a cup filled with dried tea and I just said, 'Do you think I could get a drop of water with it?'

It got a huge laugh, but during the interval, I went up to Sid and said, 'I'm ever so sorry, but I just felt it was a good line.' Sid said not to apologise and anything I wanted to add in, I should. He said, 'You're a very good actor and I'm a very good reactor, so you say that line and I'll react to it, and we'll get another laugh.'

I did a summer season every year and a panto every year after that.

John would go to London and he moved in with Ken to be nearer the theatres and be available if and when more noticeable parts came up.

A mutual friend of Barry Howard's and John's – Paul Mead – recalls how he became part of a regular get-together when John and his partner Ken moved south to work. He said:

I was friends with Barry from Murdella Grammar School in Nottingham – he lived about half a mile away from me. I was a bit older than Barry and his dad owned the butchers near to my house.

I didn't know him that well at school, but the first time we met was when I was in the company at Nottingham Playhouse, and he joined – it was his first job after leaving Birmingham Theatre School and he was in a play called *The Shoemaker's Holiday*. In this business, you meet people and then you don't see them for years – but when you do, you pick up where you left off.

I first met John in 1962 because a friend of mine called Anthony Linford was in the company with him at Chelmsford and when he wasn't working, they used to have Friday night Monopoly sessions at John and Ken's flat in Notting Hill Gate along with Gerald Moon and I was just sort of introduced and integrated into that. Ken was an actor as well – he was older than John and he eventually went to live in South Africa. That continued each week for a couple of years, and they went on from 8 p.m. to midnight. We'd have cheap booze because none of us had any money and remember John was struggling for work at the time.

That ended when John went on tour with Barry on a *Salad Days* tour which did extremely well – a play which I choreographed, played almost every role in and lived off for a year! John was very funny, especially when he was with Barry.

After the successes of *What a Racket* and another play he'd appeared in called *Friends and Neighbours*, *Salad Days* would prove John Inman's biggest hit yet. The move south had been a wise one, and things were definitely moving in the right direction, if not quite at the speed he wanted. However, he was getting noticed – and earning more substantial roles as he went along.

The gamble to leave menswear behind had most definitely paid off.

3

Salad Days, Indeed

Arthur Lane's production of *Salad Days* kept John Inman and Barry Howard in salad and much grander fayre for the best part of eighteen months as it toured up and down the land to packed houses. John played PC Boot in the musical, which also featured Patricia Duggan, Belinda Carroll and Noelle Finch – the latter would become one of John's closest friends over the years to come.

The Inman–Howard partnership had also led to a lucrative panto opportunity, as they performed alongside one another as the Ugly Sisters in *Cinderella* – but also appeared together in *Babes in the Wood*, *Mother Goose* and *Aladdin*. They had quickly established themselves as the best panto double act in the business and were in high demand around the country for their festive hijinks.

Costume designer Peter Richards first met John in 1965 and paints a picture of what the talented entertainer's life was like at the time:

John was performing the musical *Salad Days* in the mid-1960s. A friend of mine called Malcolm was a reporter on the weekly Brentford & Chiswick newspaper and he used to get free tickets to the first night or the second night of any new shows that were opening in or around London to go along and review them.

I was living in Kensington at the time and was passionate about the theatre, so I would go along with him and watched any number of plays, shows and musicals in the West End whenever I could. One of them, *Salad Days*, was touring at the time and it was opening at the New Lyric in Hammersmith.

Malcolm had a friend, the actor Ken Parry, who had been in a lot of TV and films. Ken said he had a few friends in *Salad Days* and asked why we didn't go and see them after the show? I wasn't keen on going if I'm completely honest – I don't know why – but we went to see *Salad Days* in Hammersmith all the same.

I enjoyed the show immensely, but there was no stage door at the New Lyric at that time, so we didn't bother meeting Ken's friends. A few weeks later, Malcolm called again and asked if I'd like to go and see *Salad Days* again and suggested that this time we would make an effort to go and meet Ken's friends, who happened to be John Inman and Barry Howard. We met up after the show and all got along really well.

John said that he was living in Bayswater, which wasn't far from where I was living, so we agreed to meet up the following Tuesday at a pub that was easy for us all to get to. So we did, and we had a pleasant evening out, enjoyed a few drinks and swapped showbiz stories, but that was that and we said goodbye and thought no more of it.

A week later, Malcolm and I were in the same pub and the doors opened and there was John and Barry smiling – they came over to us, we picked up from the previous week and that would became a regular thing we ended up calling 'Club Night'.

The pub was always quiet on a Tuesday so we could meet up, chat, and have a few pints of Guinness and it was all very nice. Many years earlier, I had fallen in love with Blackpool because the first time I arrived at Central Station, I walked down the high street and I looked to my right and there was the Queen's Theatre, to my left there was the Palace Theatre and the Blackpool Tower, and I became smitten with the place from that moment on. I'd go and stay in a bed and breakfast every year and, of course, that's where John's mum and dad had bought their own guest house on Bank Street.

I got on with John immediately and because comedy was my first love and I had seen so many shows, we chatted about the business, actors and, of course, I knew Blackpool so well – it seemed to have a theatre on every corner at that time – plus I knew the shows and comedy actors that had played there. So we had a lot in common and we just fell in love with each other, as friends, and that's how it started, and I'm privileged to say I became one of his closest friends for the rest of his life.

A role in *How Now Brown Cow* at the Lyric Theatre in 1965 was followed by various panto appearances and other roles that were all enjoyable and paid for his food and lodgings, but John still hadn't had the one that catapulted him into the public eye.

What he needed was television work and later that year, he landed a part in the TV series *A Slight Case of …*, appearing in the third episode of season 1, entitled 'The Enemy Within', with Roy Kinnear and Joe Melia the main protagonists and also featuring an appearance by Jon Pertwee.

A year later and he was offered the opportunity to work with producer David Croft for the first time. Again, it would initially be a minor role in a comedy series called *Hugh and I*, but it would keep John in Croft's mind for future opportunities.

He appeared in season 5's episode 4, 'Goodbye Dolly', and although it was the briefest of cameos, his delivery made Croft smile and he was asked back for episode 9 of the same season, 'It's in the Stars'. The stars of the show were Terry Scott and Hugh Lloyd, and the series would run for five years, with Mollie Sugden appearing in thirty-three of the sixty-nine episodes and, interestingly, Wendy Richard featuring in four shows and Frank Thornton in another. Although none of them appeared alongside John, all four actors would remain firmly stored in Croft's mind.

Peter Richards recalls:

John's part in *Hugh and I* was minor, and he only had one line. He was booked to play a removal man and his one line was, 'Mind your backs' and with that voice, he still got a laugh with that one sentence. He had a knack of making whatever he did, no matter how seemingly insignificant, memorable.

The loss of John's father in 1967 was a shock to the Inman family, with Frederick aged only 57. It left John's mother Mary, also 57, a widow at a relatively young age, although she would continue to live in Blackpool, where she and her husband had found their spiritual home.

Brother Geoff and a support network rallied around Mary and John travelled back for the funeral, but his mother insisted he continued with his work and return to London as soon as possible. By coincidence, he would soon be back in Blackpool working for the summer months.

John's next appearance on TV was later that year, but again it proved an underwhelming part as his minor role as the Gatekeeper in another Croft production was seen by just a handful of viewers, thanks to unfortunate scheduling. Peter Richards recalled:

I was a regular visitor to John's house by this time, stopping by almost every day before heading off to theatre to work after a couple of gin and tonics – which John poured very nicely – and we just sat and talked about the business and what was happening, and it was wonderful – he was just wonderful.

John had been doing a summer season with Sid James in Blackpool called *Wedding Fever* when he got a call from David Croft, who told him he'd enjoyed his cameos in *Hugh and I* and was directing a TV version of Gilbert and Sullivan's *Mikado* called *Titipu*, which was to go out on Boxing Day and that he had one or two parts that he felt John would be perfect for. Of course, John accepted – who wouldn't? David knew he was talented and could do it so everything was agreed.

It was recorded in September, and it was aired on Boxing Day 1967, so I went and had a belated Christmas dinner with John and watched the *Titipu* afterwards, but it went out on BBC 2 and was up against a really popular variety show called *Christmas Night With the Stars* and then, after that, *The Ken Dodd Christmas Show*, so I think we were the only ones watching it!

After that, John, who was by then back in panto, travelled back up to the Gaumont Theatre in Doncaster to continue with Barry Howard in *Cinderella*.

Work was still sporadic, but the George and Alfred Black production of *Wedding Fever* with Sid James ensured 1968 was reasonably comfortable for John. The show had been a sizeable success in Blackpool and the latest venue was the Pavilion Theatre in Torquay, where it would play to more packed houses for four months.

If John felt that this was as high profile as his career would get, nobody could have blamed him. It had been steady progress, but not meteoric and he still hadn't made it to the West End. That was until he got yet another call from David Croft, who had only been able to give John the odd small part over the past couple of years, but immensely enjoyed his performances. He had made a mental note to consider John for future productions he thought he might work well in and now he had another opportunity for the lad from Blackpool.

Based on H.G. Wells' best-selling novel, *Ann Veronica*, the story of a progressive, rebellious young woman determined to make her mark in an oppressive society, was to perform at the Cambridge Theatre, where Croft had a role for John if he was interested. Again, it would be fairly insubstantial, playing an unnamed waiter, but it was guaranteed paid work and the chance to finally realise a boyhood dream by treading the boards in the West End. He took the part, the musical ran from April to June 1969 and was a huge success.

John was intelligent and knew that by accepting these small parts, he was paying his dues with the prolific screenwriter, producer and director Croft, who by then was the darling of the BBC, having created the ratings monster that was *Dad's Army* just a year earlier. Croft was fiercely loyal to the actors he felt were reliable and were there when he needed them. In John, he envisaged bigger and better things for an actor who had made a knack of being memorable for even the briefest of appearances.

In a 1996 Radio 2 interview, John recalled:

David had given me parts – silly little, piddly parts. And then I did this musical for him in the West End called *Ann Veronica*, which he quite liked and after he wrote me a letter afterwards which said 'Dear John, thank you for your work in *Ann Veronica*, you've been very good and one day I am going to cast you in a role you can really get your teeth into, love David. PS – this letter does not constitute a contract!' I still have it.

Ann Veronica had first tried out in Coventry and that was where Jeffrey Holland – the future Spike in Croft and Jimmy Perry's hit BBC sitcom *Hi-De-Hi!* – first met John, who, in years to come, would become a co-host on a radio show called *Inman and Friends*. Holland remembered:

John came to the Belgrade Theatre in Coventry in 1969 in the first outing of the musical *Ann Veronica* starring Dorothy Tutin.

I was in the working rep company at the time, and it was a nice break for us to have a visiting company in. I don't think I said more than two words to John as our paths didn't really cross. I do remember David being very impressed with how John made the most out of what little he had been asked to do.

With *Ann Veronica*'s run over, John then reunited with *Carry On* star Sid James again, appearing in a four-month run of *His Favourite Family* at the Grand Theatre in Blackpool, before the Bernard Delfont farce journeyed to Torquay's Pavilion Theatre for another lengthy stay. Jack Douglas would take over from Sid James for the final week so he could film *Carry On Up the Jungle*.

The fact that John now had an agent, Bill Roberton, who also represented many of the *Carry On* stars and was also Jack Douglas' brother, certainly helped. Roberton was a theatre director with many show business tendrils that would ensure his client was rarely out of work.

With panto to come, once again alongside his partner in crime Barry Howard – and also Roy Castle – 1969 had arguably been John's most successful year to date. In 1970 he briefly made another TV appearance in the Sid James sitcom *Two in Clover* for ITV, playing an unnamed bowler in a cricket team run by Freddie Trueman who were taking on James' Vicar's XI. He would spend much of that year in *A Funny Thing Happened on the Way to the Forum* at the Leicester Phoenix before resuming panto with Barry Howard in *Cinderella* at the Wimbledon Theatre to see out the year with typical flamboyance.

The following year would be a difficult one, with only the odd job here and there, meaning most of John's income came from his outstanding needlework skills, repairing and creating costumes for various shows around the capital. At a time when he had needed to move up to the next level, he had endured the most barren twelve months of his career to date and was forced to question whether he'd ever get that elusive break that would jettison him from playing bit parts, sidekicks and feeding the lead actor laugh lines to something he could achieve his own fame with.

It looked an unlikely prospect at that point and there was also personal heartbreak to come because his long, very private relationship with Kenneth Hendel was also about to come to an end, with Hendel frustrated at his own slow career progression. He had been touring in a play called *Wait Until Dark* for almost two years and the relationship had been under strain for some time, so when Hendel was offered the chance to reprise his role in the production in South Africa, he accepted, hoping to start a completely new life in every sense, in a new country.

John's friends rallied around him and he was grateful to appear alongside panto 'sister' Barry Howard, who ensured there would be plenty of laughs in their annual reunion on stage in *Cinderella* alongside TV magician David Nixon, impressionist Mike Yarwood and Basil Brush at the Coventry Theatre. And he was also handed an unexpected opportunity to appear on a BBC television show he adored, *The Good Old Days*, which was a late-night variety programme set in the City Varieties Music Hall in Leeds, filmed in front of an audience wearing period clothing. A series of sketches and songs were performed by a variety of entertainers, evoking a bygone age, and John would appear in a festive special aired on Christmas Day evening, 1971.

It was his most prominent television appearance yet and it was just the fillip he needed as he faced what, on paper, was another bleak year with no work of any substance planned in the months ahead other than costume design and repair. There was always the possibility of returning to Austin Reed, who would have welcomed him back in a heartbeat, but while working in a gents' outfitters most certainly wasn't what John wanted to do next, it was, ironically, what writer David Croft had in mind for him.

Croft and Jeremy Lloyd had written a one-off programme for the BBC's Comedy Playhouse, and Croft felt he finally had a part that would give John the opportunity to really shine, as well as other actors he'd worked with in the past such as Wendy Richard, Mollie Sugden, Frank Thornton and a rising young actor on ITV called Trevor Bannister.

Croft sent the script to Coventry for John, who was wrapping up the latest *Cinderella* panto, to look over, adding a note that he'd be playing Mr Humphries in a show set in the fictional department store, Grace Brothers. He asked if he'd be interested in taking the part.

With no projects scheduled and the panto due to end in a few days' time, he was indeed very interested, and John Inman's life was about to change forever.

4

Are You Free, Mr Inman?

Britain in 1972 was a depressing place to be.

A miners' strike frequently made headline news, power cuts regularly left households and communities in darkness, plus there was rubbish piled high on the streets as refuse collectors joined a host of different public sector operatives in taking industrial action as unemployment topped 1 million for the first time in forty years. A national state of emergency was called by the government because the country was in a spiralling mess, with poverty and homelessness on the increase and strikes affecting almost every area of daily life.

Terrorism was rife at home and abroad and there seemed little cause for optimism as the free-wheeling, free love, hippy-tastic days of the 1960s disappeared quickly in the rearview mirror. If ever people needed escapism, it was now.

John Inman had by this time turned 37 and was reflective on his achievements. He'd spent the past decade working steadily around the country in various theatrical comedies and pantos, but the truth was that while his West End debut in *Ann Veronica* may have garnered positive notices, it had done little to project him into the public eye. He could have been forgiven for wondering if his chance hadn't passed him by as he approached his forties.

But everything was about to change, though it would take a bizarre and tragic turn of events to really kickstart his career on the small screen. In a 1993 US TV interview, John recalled:

> It had been three years since *Ann Veronica*, and I was doing a show in Coventry. We were about to finish our run and a couple of days before we did, a script arrived in the post from David Croft asking if I wanted to be in a Comedy Playhouse on the BBC – it was a one-off show and was for one week's work and it came with a little note from David saying: 'Dear John, would you like to do this and would you like to play Mr Humphries, who is the second sales on the gentleman's hosiery dept?' and I thought, 'Yes, of course John would like to because John was out of work in a few days' time'.

Close friend Peter Richards remembered the enthusiasm John had for the project, adding:

> I was at his flat at Ladbroke Gardens and he told me he'd got a call from David Croft to attend a meeting because he wanted him to appear in a Comedy Playhouse he was making. He went along and John told me it was about a shop and if the BBC liked it, they might commission a series, so he was quite excited about that.

The premise for the show was based on the experiences of the other half of the writing team, Jeremy Lloyd, who had worked for Simpsons of Piccadilly in London for a time. Lloyd had been away for several years working in America with a degree of success on *Rowan & Martin's Laugh-In*, though incredibly, fate had seen him reluctantly turn down an invitation to spend the evening with actress Sharon Tate and friends – on the very night they were horrifically murdered by the delusional followers of Charles Manson – and he had since returned to the UK.

Lloyd had been desperate to create a sitcom of some sort and really make his mark on home soil, and it was during his brief marriage to aspiring actress Joanna Lumley in 1970 that she'd convinced him to make something of all the stories he told her he'd experienced while working for Simpsons of Piccadilly. So he set about writing about the many mishaps and adventures he'd had during that period of his life, and after teaming up with David Croft, the pair had a half-hour script for a BBC pilot.

It would feature an ensemble cast, set on a floor within the fictional Grace Brothers department store where the men's outfitters were forced to share with the women's outfitters, to be filmed on one set in front of a live studio audience.

'After accepting, I went along to the rehearsal the following week and I was the only person I'd never heard of!' recalled John. 'There was Mollie Sugden, Frank Thornton, Trevor Bannister, and Wendy Richard – all of whom I'd seen on TV regularly – so I knew all these people, but they didn't know me.'

Bannister had been poached by the BBC after his successful stint on *The Dustbinmen*, which had been a ratings winner for ITV. He would later reveal he was sold the idea of a possible series called *Are You Being Served?* as a vehicle to make him a star on the BBC and his involvement was quite a coup for Croft and Lloyd. All the cast had connections to the writing team in some form or other, and the read through for the pilot episode proved the casting had been excellent, with an immediate camaraderie forming among a very experienced group of actors that also included the imitable Arthur Brough, Nicholas Smith and Larry Martyn.

The play was to be filmed in black and white and though John's character would be noticeable, he didn't have that many lines. However, with typical delivery skill, what he did say was memorable and got some of the best laughs from the live audience.

Tony Hare, who would go on to write for many BBC comedy shows on TV and radio, was present during filming of the Comedy Playhouse special, not imagining that he would one day end up writing regularly for John:

I was working as an assistant floor manager in television and was writing comedy material as well. I worked on the pilot of *Are You*

Being Served?, which is where I first met John. My agent knew John's agent – Bill Roberton – who also represented a lot of the *Carry On* film stars.

Bill was at the pilot filming and my main job was to look after the performers and get them to the floor in time for their shots. I introduced myself to John, who seemed like a really nice guy, we filmed the pilot and that was that.

I just loved David Croft's writing and casting, and everyone was brilliant in it.

There were several lines in the script of 'Are you free?' dispersed among the cast, but when Mr Humphries was asked if he was free for the first time, he looked over his shoulder and then replied, 'Yes, at the moment.'

Filming was completed, editing finished and the Comedy Playhouse entitled *Are You Being Served?* was readied for future broadcast, but without a specific date to air.

In fact, the general reaction at the BBC was lukewarm at best, with no guarantee it would be aired. The saucy postcard dialogue set into the seemingly uninteresting backdrop of a department store didn't excite entertainment executives, who felt the smutty jokes would be better served on ITV. Thames, in particular, was suggested at executive meetings as a better home for comedy of that ilk – off the record, of course. Such was the general disdain that there was the very real possibility the pilot episode would never see the light of day at all.

John had returned to his home town Blackpool to appear in a summer season of *The Love Nest* with Jack Douglas, and it was during this time that his personal life was turned upside down as he met the man he would spend the rest of his life with – Ron Lynch. Peter Richards remembers:

John was doing a summer season at the Blackpool Grand and one evening theatrical impresario Bernard Delfont had arranged a big supper and cabaret event for the leading actors.

Among the 'turns' was a magician on ice – don't ask! – and John was introduced to him after the show. An immediate spark was struck, and a fling developed. I went up to see the play a few weeks later but it was a very depressing weekend because 'lover-boy' had just told John that he had found someone else.

John was extremely upset as he'd obviously not long come out of a relationship with Kenneth Hendel. Later in the season, John went to another after show dinner/cabaret, which included another magician! His heart sank, believing it would be the same act and same assistant, but thankfully, this magician wasn't on ice and was just a regular chap with a side-kick. That side-kick was Ron Lynch, who was a local lad from Fylde. He was very handsome, in his mid-20s, I'd guess, and I think they fell for each other more or less as soon as they met.

They began to see each other regularly and were soon inseparable. At the end of the season Ron up-anchored and set off for London to join John. Ron also earned a bit working for Social Services, but John soon suggested that he pack that up and become his manager.

And as John's personal life took an upturn, so did his professional life, with the pilot for *Are You Being Served?* finally about to be aired in the most unlikely and tragic set of circumstances.

Viewers around world were gripped by dramatic televised events unfolding at the 1972 Munich Olympic Games, which had begun on 5 September. Eight members of the terrorist organisation Black September had invaded the athletes' compound and were holding the Israeli Olympians hostage in their apartment complex, killing two in a bloody battle to overpower them.

The games were suspended as the hostage situation grew more grave by the hour, with live news coverage of the terrorists' demands – the release of 234 Palestinian prisoners – along with a warning that if these were not met in the timescale they had outlined, there would be grave consequences. The German authorities used delaying tactics to try to hatch a rescue plan, but they were sadly very much out of their depth.

Events were about to take an horrific turn and after the terrorists negotiated a flight from Munich Airport to any Arab country in a Boeing 737, the Black September members became suspicious of the bus that would transport them from the athletes' village to the airport and so demanded two helicopters instead. The bus journey was the planned ruse for a rescue attempt by the German special forces, who now had to quickly rethink their operation.

The terrorists and the Israeli athletes arrived at Munich Airport in helicopters, but when two of the Black September members inspected the waiting – but empty – aircraft, they realised they were being set up. Sensing they had moments to live, they ran back to the helicopters, where they shot and blew up their captives in a horrific conclusion to the siege. A total of seventeen people lost their lives.

It is almost impossible to link that massacre with a light entertainment programme in Britain, but the fact was that the pilot episode of *Are You Being Served?* had been gathering dust at the BBC and it was as a direct result of events in Munich that the show was finally screened. The BBC's blanket coverage of the Olympics was paused as IOC officials met to decide whether to call the Games off completely, but while they did, the BBC still had a schedule to fulfil and in a desperate search for programmes to fill the void, the unused *Are You Being Served?* was perfect to fill at least one half-hour slot. So, on Friday, 8 September 1972, Mr Humphries, Mrs Slocombe, Captain Peacock and the rest of the characters were introduced to the British public for the very first time.

'I was highly delighted it was finally being screened because I thought it was the most wonderful thing,' said John in later years. 'But David Croft told us not to read the papers the next day because we'd be very upset with the reviews. And he was right – the critics hated it. They thought it was old, dreary, and said things like, "Who wants to look at people in a shop?"'

Despite the negativity, Croft and Lloyd could sniff a series and met with the new head of light entertainment, Bill Cotton, to discuss the possibility of making more. There had been a certain snobbishness towards *Are You Being Served?* – a sort of 'the BBC don't make these sorts of comedies', which they compared unfavourably with one of ITV's biggest hits *On the Buses*, which was drawing in millions of viewers.

But Croft was held in high esteem at the BBC. The creator of corporation favourite *Dad's Army* could do no wrong and, as Cotton had discovered that another sitcom project was lagging well behind schedule, Croft convinced him to give *Are You Being Served?* a chance by promising to deliver a complete series within six weeks and on a minimal budget.

Cotton agreed to five more episodes – with one caveat. 'OK, if you can deliver it, we'll have some of those,' he told Croft, adding – famously – 'but get rid of the poof.'

In an exchange that has since become the stuff of legend in sitcom land and recounted many times, Croft replied, 'Well, if the poof goes, I go.' Croft – and the poof – stayed.

Filming began shortly after, with David Croft and John Inman very much on board. 'I was back in Blackpool playing Jack Douglas' father-in-law in a show and I got a call from David saying, "I think we're going to do another five episodes, are you interested?" And of course, I was,' recounted John.

There was still time to squeeze in a couple of jobs before returning to London, one being a week of appearing in the ugly duckling-themed play *My Fat Friend* at the Rex Theatre in Wilmslow, Cheshire, where he would replace Kenneth Williams, who was unwell. There was also a role in a farce in London that would see him reunite with the husband of old friend Christine Ozanne. She recalled:

Of course, I'd worked with Kenneth Hendel in 1961, and John in 1962. I then toured with John and Charlie Chester, and did rep at Chelmsford with him [Kenneth] and after seeing John in *See How they Run* with me in Chelmsford, in which he played a highly comical vicar called the Reverend Humphries!

Because of that, my husband, Patrick Tucker, thought John would be perfect for the very camp part in *Boys in the Band* that he was directing, and it proved to be a great production. John was amazing, but during the rehearsals the theatre producer Freddie Piffard was watching and took Patrick to one side and said, 'What exactly is this? I thought it was a musical. You can't put that out!' But it was a huge success.

John was an incredible costume designer and could improvise with props, and I remember he made me a birdcage with a canary in about ten minutes out of wire coat hangers and what not during a musical in Chelmsford.

Then it was off to play panto, once again appearing with partner in crime Barry Howard as the nation's favourite Ugly Sisters at the Bristol Hippodrome over Christmas and New Year before filming began on the additional five episodes of the Croft and Lloyd sitcom that were to be broadcast starting in March 1973.

But *Are You Being Served?* would have yet more obstacles to clear, with the schedulers airing the first episode on Wednesday, 21 March at 7.30 p.m. – in direct competition with ITV's flagship soap *Coronation Street*, which regularly attracted in excess of 20 million viewers. It meant ratings were poor, and with no option to tape record the programme for viewers (video recorders being several years off and BBC iPlayer just a distant dream), it largely flew under the radar of the watching nation. The BBC's obvious disregard for the show was clear, and it was as though executives almost wanted it to fail. But it at least had some friends in high places, no doubt due to Croft's golden-boy reputation, as it would get another chance to prove itself – something many sitcoms weren't afforded the luxury of.

During a US TV interview, John recalled in 1993:

After the initial run, the BBC, in their wisdom, which they actually had back then, decided to put the first series out again a little while later, but this time on a Friday evening, including the pilot episode, which made for a six-week run – and it suddenly went through the roof. Everyone wanted to see it and the BBC then wanted to make more and more.

When Mr Humphries first came on the screen, I became a star overnight – after twenty years! And it was true. I'd been working very hard for twenty years and enjoying every minute of it, but suddenly I'd become famous and viewers thought I'd just appeared from nowhere!

With 12 million viewers tuning into the new Friday night slot, the true public appeal of *Are You Being Served?* had been realised and, whether the executives and men in suits upstairs liked it or not, they had a hit on their hands and a second series was duly commissioned.

Co-writer Jeremy Lloyd's former wife Joanna Lumley was an unknown young actress but would make a brief appearance in episode 4, 'His & Hers', and recalled, 'It was a sheer delight to work with John Inman: he was very clever and professional and extremely kind to me, a lowly guest artist who thought the world of his work.'

There was still time to squeeze in a seven-week nationwide tour of the play *Pyjama Tops* between September and December 1973 before yet another stint with Barry Howard as the Ugly Sisters in *Cinderella* at the Palace Theatre in Manchester.

Being on a popular sitcom had raised John's profile to unprecedented levels and he was ensuring he made the most of it, as there was still a general feeling around *Are You Being Served?* suggesting that the top brass at the BBC would cancel the show at the first opportunity, despite its popularity. Croft and Lloyd could see the potential in Mr Humphries' camper than camp character and set about making what had been a supporting role into a starring one as they sat down to write the next season. They knew they had to make the second series even better than the first if they were to avoid the dreaded 'cancelled' letter from upstairs …

5

Carry on Camping

If *Are You Being Served?* had genuinely been intended as a vehicle to further Trevor Bannister's career, this very talented and versatile actor was very quickly overshadowed by the antics of Mollie Sugden and John Inman's scene-stealing performances in the show. Croft and Lloyd had identified both Mrs Slocombe and the effeminate Wilberforce Claybourne Humphries as the characters who were getting the biggest laughs from the audience, and so ensured they would get the best lines going forward.

Sugden had worked with Croft at length in the series *Hugh and I*, but John's cameos had only scratched the surface of his comedic talents and timing, and by series 2 he was already one star, if not *the* star, of the show. And while his character never professed to be gay, his camp demeanour, self-proclaimed 'mincing walk' and endless innuendos actually made him the most prominent (alleged) homosexual on British TV at the time.

In many respects, it was a landmark moment for sitcoms in this country and John, who admitted that most of the time he was very much playing himself, was creating a discussion in homes up and down the land and raising awareness that perhaps some people were just different.

The equally camp Larry Grayson was also emerging as a house-wives' favourite, with Larry and John's portrayals being a natural progression from Kenneth Williams' many camp roles in the *Carry On* movies and Frankie Howerd's 'Shut your face!' stand-up routine. None of the quartet were openly gay in their personal lives, with Grayson, Howerd and Williams considered almost asexual in many ways and John claiming new boyfriend Ron was actually his manager and PA, which in fairness was a role he was fulfilling.

The cast quickly became tight knit, with John particularly close to Wendy Richard and Mollie Sugden, though there were no divisions in what was very much a happy and contented ensemble. During an interview with WLIW 21 in the USA, John recalled:

Mr Humphries started older and got younger as he went along. From four lines in the pilot, he was written up and written up. We were like a family. Arthur Brough was a beautiful man, and he was sort of the daddy of the cast – he was irreplaceable, even though they tried many times over the years.

Each morning when I had rehearsals with Trevor and Arthur for our scenes, Arthur would look at his watch and then whisper to us both, 'It's 11 a.m. you know, and the hostelry is open. Now this is just for medicinal purposes only, I'm just going away for a little while' – and he would disappear from the room! We'd have to use delaying tactics on the script read through, like 'Would this work better if I said it?' or whatever until Arthur waddled back in having had his pink Plymouth gin – he was really sweet and a lovely, lovely man. I don't think David Croft realised what had been happening for quite some time until this one occasion when it was pouring with rain outside and when Arthur returned, he was soaked to the skin. David said, 'You old rascal – you've been in the bloody pub!' It was hilarious.

Peter Richards, who had been in show business in one form or another for more than three decades and would be part of the studio audience at each and every recording of the show, remembered:

Are You Being Served? was very cheap to make as it was all filmed on one set – like *Steptoe and Son* – there's no outside filming involved, the main set was that of a department store floor, some stairs with a lift at the top and a side setting for the canteen and Mr Rumbold's office and that was it.

The ratings for the first series hadn't been that good, but the decision to repeat all six episodes on Friday evenings had been a wise one and because it was inexpensive to make and quick, they'd of course decided to do another five episodes. This time, the second series went out after *The Generation Game* on a Saturday evening and suddenly the viewing figures went through the roof.

The second season ran from 14 March to 11 April 1974. Mr Humphries featured noticeably more than he had in the first series, finally making the 'I'm free!' catchphrase his own and creating one of British sitcom's most remembered and recognisable sayings in the process.

Of course, that line was no more than a statement of availability, but in John Inman's capable hands it became a comedic line that guaranteed big laughs each and every time. Peter Richards continues:

It's funny because in the pilot episode, it was Mollie who said the line 'I'm free', first, but John told me that on the way back to the dressing rooms, someone asked where John was and he shouted, 'I'm free!' from the back and everyone laughed. Mollie – what a lovely, unselfish woman she was – went to see David Croft and said she thought John should have that line – and he agreed, so as they went along, 'I'm free!' became John's catchphrase, and the rest is history!

Fame and fortune overnight – the sort that, as John often pointed out, in reality had taken more than twenty years to achieve – was in his grasp. He lived a very comfortable life before *Are You Being Served?* but things were about to move to a different sphere and the likeable and unassuming actor was suddenly in high demand for interviews, chat shows and the offers of work were flooding in.

TV ratings were nudging 15 million and John's diary soon filled for months ahead – including the commission of a third series of *Are You Being Served?* The new season was slated for the start of 1975 and would run for nine episodes – four more than season 1 and 2, which had been five each (not including the Comedy Playhouse pilot). The men in suits might not have liked the show, but they weren't stupid – *Are You Being Served?* was by now one of the country's most popular shows and John Inman was a bankable star.

He would need to juggle his schedule, too, with filming for the new series in February 1975 conflicting with his role in the 'sensuous sex comedy' *Let's Get Laid* – which John told his mother was about life on a chicken farm! The so-called 'King of Soho', nightclub owner and erotic entrepreneur Paul Raymond had acquired the Windmill Cinema and returned it to a theatre for the first time in a decade in order to host his often risqué shows.

Let's Get Laid was the first show at the restored venue and would run from September 1974 to June 1976. It was an enormous success and starred Fiona Richmond, Victor Spinetti and Jenny Kenna, with John playing Gordon Hardcastle. He stayed in the twice-nightly show for fourteen months – give or take breaks for filming or other obligations – before being replaced by Brian Marshall due to work commitments and what had become a relentless schedule.

Filming for season 3 of *Are You Being Served?* began on Friday, 21 February 1975, with an incredibly quick turnaround in order to air the following Thursday. The third series proved the most popular yet, with close on 20 million viewers tuning in regularly to watch the staff of Grace Brothers and their various adventures on the shop floor.

There was also a first Christmas special – one of three filmed during the show's twelve-year run, entitled 'Christmas Crackers', and it was here that the world was first introduced to bolshy canteen manageress Diana Yardswick, played by former Tiller Girl Doremy Vernon.

She recalled:

I remember my first scene when I had to put the plates down in the canteen. I was so scared because I'd left Rep to work on the show and when I saw I only had two words of dialogue – 'plates' and 'elbows', I was so angry that I threw the plates down in front of the cast and they initially looked stunned, but then they roared with laughter, which helped to get me some laughs early!

I joined for the third series. David Croft always got together a perfect cast and I remember Mollie had been huge on radio and she could do a read though perfectly and she was undoubtedly the star at the time. On the credits as the show began, Trevor was second bill, but John became third bill – and then he overtook Trevor and eventually would share top billing with Mollie.

I learned later that there were initially tiny factions among the cast, but after the first series, they knitted together really well. When I was given the part, they were very welcoming towards me. I had worked with John before at Rep in Leicester when he was what's described as a 'jobbing actor' and I'd known he was quite close with Barry Howard, so while I was unknown among the others, I knew John already, which really helped.

It was great fun. We started with a read through and if the regulars didn't get a laugh when they read their lines, David Croft would cut the line. John was very gregarious and helped me settle in quickly, and he was very close to Wendy Richard. After each rehearsal, they would head off to the pub together at twelve o'clock. They drank champagne together and John would buy her bottles of the stuff because she demanded it!

We rehearsed at the BBC's Acton Rehearsal Rooms on Acton Road. There were seventeen rooms where all kinds of shows were being rehearsed and on our rehearsal days, we'd all arrive in the morning and because we were lazy, we would eat when we got there and have breakfast together in this wonderful canteen they had. I remember a producer joining us one day, but leaving half his food when he got up and left and John said,

'You can tell he wasn't a war baby.' He was just witty with perfect timing, no matter what the situation was, it was just a talent that he had.

Recordings would be in front of a live studio audience of about 300 people, which was never easy. In rehearsals and read throughs, you'd learn the lines and know where the laughs were, but when it was filmed, you needed to get it right because David Croft didn't like to stop filming because he felt the laugh from the audience was never the same on a second or third take, so there was a lot of pressure to deliver.

We had a warm-up guy before each recording, but he wasn't very funny. John could have done that as he would have had them in stitches. They would introduce the cast to the audience at the beginning, starting with lowly characters like me, and build up to either Mollie or John, and they would alternate them both. The star always comes last and that's why I think Mollie and John's salary was on a par at the time.

John was never less than hilarious and on one occasion, a transexual friend from Manchester had written to me to say she used to play with John as kids when he lived in Blackpool, and she'd provided this photo of herself as she was now with her legs wide open – it was very funny. I brought the picture to rehearsals and said to John, 'Now this is a transexual who specialises in bondage and humiliation, and she says she used to play with you, do you remember her?' and he just took a look at the photo, saw she had a hole in her knickers and said, 'Well, I don't know the lady.' It was his delivery that made you laugh so much.

Later, during the Friday rehearsals for the technicians and the two scriptwriters, he was walking down the stairs in Grace Brothers, and he said, 'Hello, I'm Mr Humphries, I'm in men's underwear and I specialise in bondage and humiliation.' The crew just fell about laughing.

John was already living with Ron by that stage – when I'd first met him in Leicester, he had already been doing pantomime for several years. He loved pantomime and he used to keep every costume he'd ever made in his garage at his house, and loved doing it even more than *Are You Being Served?* in my opinion.

The popularity of his catchphrase saw John invited to record his first single by DJM Records, with 'Are You Being Served, Sir?' released in October 1975. It reached No. 39 in the charts and spent six weeks in the UK Top 75, a decent showing for a novelty record. John would release an album and a couple more singles, none of which charted, but he certainly enjoyed the experience of being in a recording studio.

With his star rapidly rising and his relationship with Ron steady and calm, 1975 had been quite the year for Frederick John Inman, but it would pale into comparison to what awaited in 1976 …

6

The Nation's Favourite

The year 1976 was a golden one for John Inman.

A fourth series of *Are You Being Served?* had been commissioned with filming due to start in April of that year and would consist of seven episodes plus a second Christmas special later in the year. The production team for the show would see the addition of the highly regarded Susan Belbin, who would take on the role of assistant stage manager for season 4. Her pathway to the show was interesting, and her rise in the industry had been somewhat meteoric:

I worked in a theatre and worked my way up to be stage manager at the Scottish TV variety show *The White Heather Club* and the person who produced there was also a BBC producer called Ian MacFadyen.

I got a call one morning out of the blue from the BBC telling me I was late for work, so I said, 'Excuse me?' – the lady went on, saying I was due in 9 a.m. to start a three-week freelance job that Ian had recommended me for. Only nobody had bothered to tell me!

I'd never been in a TV studio in my life, so I walked down to Queen Margaret Drive, which was just down the road from me in Glasgow, and presented myself. I overdressed with high heels and a frock, which is the last thing you should wear in a studio because high heels pierce the floor and you're liable to trip on any number of cables and what not. Fortunately, the costume department gave me a pair of plimsoles. So it wasn't the most auspicious of starts to my career in TV but, for whatever reason, I never left TV after that and stayed in the business for many, many years.

I spent four years at BBC Scotland until my boss, Lee Ashton, called me in and said, 'Suzie, they're looking for somebody in London,' and I told him that was the last place I wanted to live and work, but he insisted I apply, and I eventually agreed to fill out an application. When I'd completed it, I took it into Lee and as he started reading it, he said, 'No, no, no ... *this* is what we'll say,' and began to rewrite the form, stating that I'd been an assistant floor manager for BBC Scotland – which I most certainly wasn't!

I applied, got an interview, and went down to London before travelling home to Glasgow. Soon after I learned I'd got the job. All my colleagues, family, and friends were asking what I'd be doing, and I said I wasn't 100 per cent certain, but I had heard Morecambe and Wise were looking for somebody – and that's exactly what I ended up doing, working with Eric and Ernie for the next three years.

They were perfectionists and they wanted everything to be word perfect before a big star walked through the rehearsal room door, and nothing was left to chance. During my time with the boys I had to play the role of the star in every rehearsal until they were ready, which, as you can imagine, was never dull! They wanted me to become their manager and said they'd set me up in a posh office in London, but I decided it was time to move on and try something new.

Then I had a conversation with a colleague called Annie, who was looking to move into variety, and I said, 'That's funny, because I'm looking to get into comedy,' and with that, we swapped places. She went to work on *Morecambe and Wise* and I went to work with David Croft.

On my first day, I tiptoed into David's office, and he said, 'Oh hello – who are you?' I explained that Annie and I had swapped places and was he OK with that? He said it was fine and that was the start of my ten years working with David Croft.

I began working on *Porridge* and when a new sitcom called *Are You Being Served?* was commissioned, I ended up working on that show, too, a few years later.

I joined the show in 1976, which was the fourth season, and they were still working very hard at making it a ratings success. John was very big at that time because I'd seen him in panto, and he was very well-known.

I became the assistant floor manager on *Are You Being Served?*, and my role was to mark out the rehearsal room, get the scripts and read through them and then it would be a case of rehearsing, marking out the floor where the cast needed to be for each scene and acquiring any props that were needed. During rehearsals, I'd be on the book [the script] and prompt the actors as and when needed.

The cast trusted David Croft implicitly, but if any of the actors thought they could add something – maybe a silly walk or reaction or whatever – they would just do it and if we saw David's shoulders going up and down, he was laughing to himself and liked it, so it would stay in. If he didn't like it, he'd just say 'stick to the script'. John was very inventive, and he knew what was funny so invariably when he came up with something, it stayed in.

The cast got on well, but I have to say Nicholas Smith was a boring so and so – he was an interesting person, but in all honesty I felt he was a little out of his depth because I don't think he was well suited to comedy. Of course, his role was more serious in the show and the other cast members were always poking fun at him when we filmed – all scripted of course.

It was a TV recording onto videotape in front of a live studio audience, who would come in between 7 to 7.30 p.m. and we'd start filming from 8 p.m. until about 10 p.m. Beforehand, we'd introduce all the characters to the audience and then Felix Bowness would be the warm-up guy at the time and then we'd start recording. We had two hours to complete each episode.

David Croft learned that I was keen to direct, so he let me do the canteen scenes with Doremy Vernon as the canteen manager. I'd been taught by the best and I was very good at watching, listening, and soaking up how it was done, and because of my background with *Morecambe and Wise* and *Porridge*; you don't get any better training than that. I had to get it right because I didn't want to let David down more than anything else.

John Inman was having the time of his life, but that year hadn't been without upset as he recovered from the shock of close friend Sid James' sudden death on stage in Sunderland aged only 62. A tireless worker, heavy smoker and drinker, James' bad habits were a reminder to John, himself a smoker, drinker and workaholic, that the demands of showbusiness mixed with an unhealthy lifestyle could prove catastrophic.

John was soon on his way back to his beloved Blackpool for another summer season – only this time he took the majority of the cast with him for the live stage version of *Are You Being Served?*, which ran from June to October 1976. It was a gruelling schedule for the cast, with performances at 7 p.m. and 9 p.m. each night (except Sunday) and it played to packed audiences throughout its long and lucrative run.

Written by Croft and Lloyd, the synopsis for the stage show read:

When the motley crew of the Grace Brothers department store prepare for a sale of German goods before departing for a staff holiday in Spain, where they survive their stay in the tropics at a one-star establishment and encounter everything from a Spanish crumpet to randy revolutionaries with everything intact but their modesty.

It was perfect for Blackpool, home of the saucy postcard, and even more so with an audience largely made up of holidaymakers, who lapped up the opportunity to see their favourite sitcom live and up close.

Edinburgh-based writer, director and broadcaster Liam Rudden, a huge fan of the show, wrote on his website, Liam Rudden Media:

In the summer of 1976, a stage adaptation of *Are You Being Served?* ran at the Winter Gardens in Blackpool. Directed by Robert Redfarn. John Inman, Mollie Sugden, Frank Thornton, Wendy Richard, and Nicholas Smith reprised their characters from the television show, while the characters of Mr Lucas and Mr Grainger were recast.

The play had basically the same plot as the film version which would debut the next year, though Young Mr Grace's role was omitted entirely, and Mr Mash had less to do than Mr Harman in the film. Reviews for the play were mixed; a writer for the Blackpool Diarist of *The Stage* declared it the funniest show he had seen in thirty years, while Michael Leapman from *The Times* declared the play to be worthless except for the final line, though he admitted he had never seen the TV version.

There was even time to squeeze a guest appearance on *The Ken Dodd Blackpool Centenary Show* along with the Goodies, which was screened on BBC1 on 19 June and recorded in the Big Top of Gerry Cottle's Circus. With a scorching heatwave lasting from mid-June to July, Blackpool's theatres, pleasure beach and beaches were packed to the rafters.

In October 1976, John travelled down to London to an event to honour his great friend Danny La Rue. The Variety Club of Great Britain were holding a star-studded luncheon to celebrate twenty-five years in showbusiness at the Savoy Hotel and he'd been asked to speak at the event. That, in turn, led to a chance for Tony Hare to work with John again for the first time since the 1973 pilot of *Are You Being Served?* Hare recalls:

A few years had passed when, Bill Roberton called me and said, 'I understand you do a bit of writing for the BBC?' – and I told him I did and that I'd had done a few things with them, and Yorkshire TV and he said, 'Good – well, John's got to do a speech for at a Variety Club luncheon as a tribute to Danny La Rue – would you like to write it?'

Of course I accepted and because I'd chatted with John in the past, I was aware he'd worked for Austin Reed's and that's where he'd worked with a floor walker he based Mr Humphries on.

So, I wrote the speech and there was one gag that went like a bomb and that was the start of me writing and working with John for the next thirty years or so. The gag? John said that Danny La Rue kept coming in Austin Reed's for suits and suchlike and he told the audience, 'And I'll never forget when I did his inside leg measurement and I'll have it hanging over my head for the rest of my life' – and with John's delivery, that got a big laugh and Danny fell about laughing.

With a *Mother Goose* panto at Wimbledon Theatre to come – his first for two years – John and Ron took a short break before it was time to go full pelt again. It was also a chance to go house hunting in London as they looked for a proper home to call their own, though it would be several months before they found the place they were looking for.

A spectacular year would end in spectacular fashion for a man who was now one of Britain's biggest stars as, he picked up a prestigious double award, first being voted the BBC Personality of the Year and then the *TV Times*' Funniest Man on Television – two huge and prestigious awards for any entertainer and a rare double in the industry. John Inman, it appeared, appealed to everybody, young and old and also both sexes. Not bad for somebody who played a very limp-wristed, effeminate counter assistant in a fictional department store.

One thing a few of John's close friends believed at the time was that Ron Lynch was keeping some people at arm's length – his long friendship with Barry Howard being one example, as Paul Mead remembers:

I'd been good friends with John for many years, until he became famous and his new boyfriend sort of cut off everybody – even Barry Howard. I was doing a performance at the Bournemouth Operatic, so I called in the town to see Barry as he was living there at the time and even he said he was finding it difficult to get to see John. They had been close for many years, playing the Ugly Sisters. They were extremely funny and good together, so I found that quite sad.

The fact that John and Barry were no longer working together in panto didn't help matters, but though Ron was almost universally liked by all who knew John, there seems to have been an element of possessiveness in his nature, particularly where his men friends were concerned. Whether he felt threatened in some way or could see things from an entirely different angle will never be known, and had John been unhappy with anything, surely he would have told Ron as much.

Peter Richards concurred with Mead, agreeing that it wasn't as simple as picking up a phone and calling John any more, with Ron fielding most calls. He said, 'Sadly, Ron had become somewhat possessive of John and "blocked" many of his friends' phone calls. I was having none of it, relying on the strength of my strong and longstanding friendship with John, but others succumbed to pressure from Ron and eventually gave up trying.'

But there would soon be an opportunity for many of John's friends to reconvene – and it would be in front of millions of TV viewers. Ahead of *Mother Goose*, there was still time to squeeze in the second *Are You Being Served?* Christmas special, which was filmed on 6 December for a Christmas Eve screening. However, during rehearsals for *Mother Goose* at Wimbledon, Eamonn Andrews surprised John by uttering those magic words, 'John Inman, this is your life'.

After being whisked to the studio for the live airing of *This is Your Life*, old friends and family were introduced along with Arthur English, who was also in the *Mother Goose* panto with John. Barry Howard, David Nixon and Roy Castle were present, as well as Mollie Sugden, Wendy Richard, Arthur Brough, Nicholas Smith and Frank Thornton. The final guest was Danny La Rue, in what was an emotional half-hour for the Lancastrian – though he had been somewhat panicky as to who would appear as guests from his past!

The comical spark between John and Barry Howard was evident as Howard, whose intro was a voiceover asking, 'Has anybody seen my sister?', recalled a panto mishap they'd shared:

It was the boudoir scene when the Ugly Sisters get ready for the ball and the management gave us a marvellous set.

We were on this bed which went back into the wall – so we did all that and John gets on the bed, says his cue, and is pulled away. I say, 'Has anybody seen my sister?' and the kids shout back 'She's gone through a hole in the wall!'

I think the lads in back stage had been out for a pint during the interval because he came back out at such a speed that he nearly knocked me over so I said, 'Ooh, you clumsy apeth and we carry on with the scene and the audience starts to laugh and we thought, 'This is going well' and then I look at John and he's laughing at me. I say, 'What are you laughing at?'

I was wearing this oversized bust and John said, 'Well, look at your tits!' I said, 'Well, what's the matter with them?' and he said, 'You've only got one!'

I turned around to look at it and I had a boob at the front and a boob at the back!

The affection and esteem Danny La Rue held John in was evident as he spoke of his friend as the final guest. He said:

I've known John since 1961 and there's nobody in our business who deserves success more. The marvellous thing about our business is we're all colleagues – there have been so many people on, I was backstage terrified thinking, 'What am I going to say?' but the one thing – thank god – nobody has said is, everybody talks about stars, but it's people who make stars and people only recognise people, and it's because you're such a marvellous person that they love you first and your character second. You're a lovely man, you're a hard worker and you're a great star, and it's my privilege to call you a friend.

It was heartfelt and emotional for John to have had such a pleasant walk down memory lane.

'It was genuinely a total surprise to John,' says Peter Richards:

He was playing Dame in panto when Eamonn Andrews strode in from the back of the stage. Once he was in the studio in his own clothes, he began to panic a bit – inwardly – wondering who they were going to bring on. To his horror they included some boys from school who he hadn't particularly wanted to keep in touch with, and men from his Austin Reed window dresser days who he was happy to see. Many of his family were there and had managed to keep it a secret, and Barry Howard and Danny, of course.

And the nation's favourite comic actor would enter lounges up and down the land yet again on Christmas Eve, first with a guest appearance on *Jim'll Fix It* singing 'Teddy Bear's Picnic' and 'Rudolph the Red Nose Reindeer' – the highlight of the episode being the attack on the now despised Jimmy Savile by Rod Hull and Emu – and then he was back on the screens a few hours later in 'The Father Christmas Affair' – the *Are You Being Served?* festive special.

Millions of viewers watched two of the top-rated shows of the year and John Inman was front and centre in both. It was the perfect footnote to a tumultuous, off the charts twelve months.

7

Onwards and Upwards

John Inman and Ron Lynch found the home of their dreams at 33 Robert Close in the Little Venice area of Maida Vale, west London. An affluent area of the capital, home to many actors, artists and celebrities, the three-storey mews house was exactly what John had been looking for as a permanent base of his own.

In 1977 it was the Queen's Silver Jubilee and also another great year for John, who would be given top billing in the movie version of *Are You Being Served?* as well as filming a fifth series of the sitcom, whose popularity continued to soar. The year would also see him get his own sitcom on ITV, *Odd Man Out*, as well as appearing again in panto. After moving into his new property, season 5 of *Are You Being Served?* was shot, aired and completed by 8 April.

Then John began preparations for principal filming of the *Are You Being Served?* movie, which would largely be based around the hugely successful stage play that had played to packed audiences in Blackpool the previous summer.

The sitcom movie spin-off was a very British phenomenon and one that had varying fortunes, too. The *On the Buses* franchise had spawned three movies – the first of which was a sizeable box office hit earning the equivalent of £41 million in today's money, but the follow-ups were less profitable.

Steptoe and Son's first movie outing took a respectable £8 million in today's money, but the follow-up, which was far superior in many ways, barely broke even at the box office. *Man About the House*, *The Likely Lads*, *Dad's Army*, *George and Mildred* ... the list is long, and few were memorable, with different sets, location filming and no studio audience often leaving the film versions feeling somewhat soulless.

Are You Being Served? had plenty going for it, with John Inman seemingly incapable of doing anything wrong in the eyes of the British public, plus the remainder of the much-loved sitcom's cast and David Croft and Jeremy Lloyd at the wheel. The BBC series was approaching its peak with 20 million viewers tuning in regularly and the stage play had been seen by many thousands of satisfied customers.

What could possibly go wrong? Well, plenty, it seems.

Are You Being Served? is not the worst film ever made, but it's a long way from the best and perhaps missed an opportunity to explore the characters more in a different environment. Taken outside of the safe, comfortable backdrop of Grace Brothers for the first time, the script felt a little lazy, with a number of jokes from earlier episodes repeated as well as one tent scene very similar to an episode in season 1.

Filming took place at Elstree Studios with a few scenes at Gatwick Airport, but the film lacked the sharpness on the small-screen version and felt little more than an extension of the *Carry On* series, which had been waning in popularity for some time. At a time when *Star Wars*, *Close Encounters of the Third Kind*, *Airport* and *Saturday Night Fever* were breaking box office records around the world, *Are You Being Served?* was the first blot on Croft and Lloyd's copybook and didn't stay in cinemas long.

Critic John Pym of the *Monthly Film Bulletin* wrote, 'The humour consists mainly of a withering selection of patent British puns; an inflatable brassiere, some let's-insult-the-Germans jokes and a rickety thunder-box that bolts from the outside are thrown in for good measure.' That pretty much summed up the general opinion, though it's fair to say diehard fans enjoyed it and in the years that have passed it has come to be viewed affectionately as a film of its time – limited, funny in parts and, of course, it was the one and only time the cast ever left their department store, so there was at least that!

John Inman's performance was up to his usual high standard, as were the rest of the cast, and it appeared not too much harm had been done to the sitcom's reputation, though the cast were about to suffer their first major loss. Arthur Brough's bumbling but lovable Mr Grainger featured in the film, but he had sadly died two months before the movie was released, just weeks after he had lost his beloved wife. His was a huge loss to the show and he deserved a better epitaph than the film version he signed off with.

If the experience of movie making had been a minor disappointment for John, his first solo TV adventure proved an even more sobering affair.

Thames Television would have loved to have got their hands on *Are You Being Served?*, but its success meant it would never leave the BBC. They settled for the next best thing – taking its star to ITV and giving him his own show. After securing a temporary release from his BBC contract, John was free to test the water with something completely different. Or at least, that's how he might have imagined it would be.

Odd Man Out was directed by Anthony Parker, who had previously worked on *My Son Reuben*, *Love Thy Neighbour* and *Mind Your Language*, with the experienced Vince Powell (*Nearest and Dearest*, *Bless this House* and *Mind your Language*) penning the scripts. Producer Gerald Thomas was a legendary figure in the world of British comedy, overseeing the *Carry On* series from 1958 to 1976, yet he only had one series of the Sid James sitcom *Bless this House* on his sitcom CV. Although Thomas' involvement had undoubtedly helped secure the services of *Carry On* legend Peter Butterworth as well as John Inman, his inexperience on the small screen, coupled with Powell's mediocre script, was a huge disappointment for the viewers.

The *British Comedy Guide*'s synopsis says:

Neville Sutcliffe leaves the familiar safety of his Blackpool fish and chip shop in order to take over the running of his late father's seaside rock factory – alongside the family he never even knew existed.

He immediately gets on the wrong side of a woman at Littlehampton train station. Unfortunately for Neville, she turns out to be his step-sister and new business partner, Dorothy! To make matters worse, the long-established family enterprise is failing. £30,000 in debt, to be precise. Can Neville save the business and fit in with his new friends, family, and staff?

Unfortunately, and despite John Inman and the cast's best efforts, nobody was that interested in what happened to Neville Sutcliffe.

Going out in a prime 9 p.m. Thursday evening slot, *Odd Man Out* missed the opportunity to show John's wide and varied breadth of comedic talent, instead producing a watered down, less catty and less funny version of Mr Humphries. Peter Richards recalled, '*Odd Man Out* was terrible. Pure slapstick and John was not happy with it – or being in it, for that matter by the time it was all over.'

The cast did their best with the tools they were given, but *Odd Man Out* fared poorly in the ratings and the seven-episode run between 27 October and 8 December was the only time Neville Sutcliffe and company were seen on British TV.

Author and critic Brian Slade, writing on the popular website Television Heaven, felt that *Odd Man Out* could have perhaps continued for at least another series, but may have been a victim of its star's success at the time. Says Slade:

Quite why *Odd Man Out* didn't continue is hard to pinpoint. The acting talent is strong and Powell, while not everyone's cup of tea, had enough experience to make a success of it. It may simply be that John Inman's character just didn't deviate far away enough from Mr Humphries at a time when *Are You Being Served?* was thriving. Neville's friend, Bobby, is clearly his significant other, although we never actually meet him, so while the camp Mr Humphries worked so well with Grace Brothers, the near carbon copy of the character never allows the viewer to see somebody else. Josephine Tewson is effective enough as Dorothy, but the real star is Butterworth, who brings all his physical comedy and gloriously pained facial expressions from the *Carry On …* films to great effect.

Once the credits have rolled, Inman addresses the audience directly to sum up the episode and to thank people for watching. It certainly adds a warmth to the show, something Inman always offered, so it's perhaps a shame that *Odd Man Out* didn't get the chance to thrive, but it represents an interesting aside within Inman's career and reminds us of just what an underrated performer Butterworth was.

At least there was panto to restore John's enthusiasm, with *Mother Goose* at the Bristol Hippodrome over Christmas and New Year. It was yet another appearance without long-time Ugly Sister Barry Howard, though the pair would never perform together again. Friends believed Howard had become increasingly bitter at John's many successes and fame and the pair rarely spoke any more. Christine Ozanne recalled:

John and Barry had had a big parting of the ways. When Barry got into *Hi-De-Hi!*, his whole personality changed completely – it was awful. He became so grand and full of himself, and John couldn't bear it. By that time, they weren't doing pantos anymore and I don't think they ever worked together again. Barry even found religion later in life. We'd got on really well because we'd toured with *Oliver!* for a year and he was so funny in a crude way.

And it wasn't only Barry Howard who had been upset with John Inman. As he prepared for a summer season in Bournemouth, he was confronted by five members of the group Campaign for Homosexual Equality, who had been picketing his show. Believing John was doing more harm to the gay community than good, they made their feelings known to the unconfrontational star, who was nonplussed as to why he'd been targeted. He commented at the time:

> They thought I was over-exaggerating the gay character. But I don't think I do. In fact there are people far more camp than Mr Humphries walking around this country.
>
> Anyway, I know for a fact that an enormous number of viewers like Mr Humphries don't really care whether he's camp or not. So far from doing harm to the homosexual image, I feel I might be doing some good.

Though Mr Humphries' sexuality was never discussed in *Are You Being Served?*, the endless innuendos and the physical behaviour of the character had, of course, been more than enough for viewers to arrive at the conclusion he was gay. Though both John and David Croft stated that the character was 'just a mother's boy', maintaining his sexual orientation was never stated explicitly, John added, 'Even when I'm not playing Mr Humphries, say at a summer season, I camp it up a bit. If I don't the audience are disappointed.'

Though we'll explore John Inman's position in either forwarding or putting the gay cause further back later in this book, he was as guarded in real life about his sexuality as he was on screen, which was, of course, completely his right. Doremy Vernon said:

> Barry Howard's friends used to ask if John was gay, and he'd tell them that he just helped them out when they needed a bit of servicing!
>
> Others would say John wasn't gay, but just outrageous. He never came out and he played his part so that people assumed he

was gay, but he was just acting in that sense. I don't know what gay people made of John – or what gay people make of other gay people because it seems to change all the time. But that walk he had – he worked hard to walk like that, and he knew he needed a catchphrase to become famous, which he got, of course.

Are You Being Served? production manager Susan Belbin agreed it was a difficult time for men to be openly gay. 'Frankie Howerd, Kenneth Williams, and Larry Grayson never admitted they were gay and in many ways were prisoners of public opinion despite their incredible popularity,' she said. 'All lived in fear of being publicly outed and the effects that may have on their career, so they remained ambiguous throughout their lives.'

Indeed, Wilfrid Brambell's randy old man character as the father in *Steptoe and Son* might never have enjoyed the success he did had he been convicted of importuning an undercover police officer in a public lavatory back in 1962. Whether viewers would have believed his frisky, 'dirty old man' persona who lusted after strippers and the young women his son Harold occasionally brought back to their hovel and scrapyard on Oil Drum Lane, had they known he was gay, is open to question. However, he was forced to claim his real-life partner was no more than his valet and had to travel to Hong Kong and the Far East in order to enjoy just being himself without judgement.

Belbin recalled:

I met Ron Lynch many times. I thought he was a lovely, lovely chap but when you're the other half of a famous person, especially in the 1970s, it can't have been easy. John was very recognisable and wouldn't have been able to walk down the street without getting stopped many times – but if he was always seen with a man, people would have started gossiping and pointing fingers because that's how it was then. So it can't have been easy for Ron, but they adored one another and he really looked after John. I remember going to a party at John's house to celebrate something or other and it was all so relaxed – nothing flashy – and it was just lovely.

So while the viewing public adored John and his portrayal of Mr Humphries, sections of the gay community did not. However, one thing was for sure: John Inman could not have cared less, because he genuinely believed some camp or even gay representation in a popular TV show was better than none at all. He was who he was, and he wasn't about to change a winning formula for anyone. One thing he was most certainly starting – perhaps for the first time in many households – was a dialogue, and one question worth asking was what might have become of *Are You Being Served?* had David Croft actually got rid of the so-called 'poof' as he'd been asked by his bosses after the pilot episode?

8

Entertaining Mr Inman

With filming for season 6 of *Are You Being Served?* not scheduled until the end of October 1978, John's diary was comparatively free, enabling him to focus on his new solo show, *Fancy Free*, for the summer seasons in Great Yarmouth and Bournemouth.

Bobby Crush, who had won talent show *Opportunity Knocks* six years earlier, was a strong support act, as were husband and wife singers Teddy Johnson and Pearl Carr. It was a variety show very much based on the vaudeville entertainers John loved so much. This meant another opportunity knocking for Tony Hare to work with John again, this time with a more substantial project that he could really get his teeth into – though he initially thought he'd blown his chance. Hare recalls:

> Bill Roberton told me he wanted to put John on the road in his own show in cabaret and would I write his act for him?
>
> I was more than happy to, and I went away and wrote quite a long piece and when I'd finished, I arranged to go and deliver the script to John at his house in Little Venice, somewhere where I'd never been before. I called around, sat down in the armchair and he made me a gin and tonic and then he also sat down and read though, it. I was sitting there thinking 'Oh my god, he hates it'

as there had been no reaction whatsoever as he studiously read my work.

Then at the end he looked up and said, 'That's great, Tony. I really like it. I'll add some of my own character to it as well,' and I said obviously, add or change [what] you want. It was a massive relief and from there on we worked together quite often.

When *Fancy Free* opened in Great Yarmouth, I missed the opening show, but I'd thought of a gag he could open the show with, so I delivered it to Ron and he passed it on to John, who liked it and thereafter started opening with the line, 'Ooh, working in Grace Brothers is such a chore,' and then started to talk about all the other characters before he ended with, 'and that Captain Peacock – what a pain he is – all Pea and ... no wonder nobody likes him!'

I would later write the sketch he performed with Henry Cooper at the Royal Variety Performance, and he introduced that measurement sketch in all his solo shows, getting a member of the audience up, which could work well if he chose the right person. In the end, we used a stooge, Raymond Bowers, who would appear in a couple of episodes of *Are You Being Served?* – just to make sure we got what we wanted out of the sketch!

Outside of the entertainment bubble, Britain was slowly recovering from the mass unemployment that had blighted the start of the 1970s, with punk rock now making the headlines and the first green shoots of alternative comedy starting to pop up in pubs and clubs around the country. Labour Prime Minister James Callaghan had called an autumn election, in which he would take on the formidable Conservative leader Margaret Thatcher – and lose heavily – but there was plenty of room for good old-fashioned family entertainment.

South coast towns such as Bournemouth, Eastbourne and Brighton were retirement hotspots where saucy, old-school comedy was warmly embraced. John had a passion for variety, and *Fancy Free* was a mixture of stories, sketches and, of course, song and dance – and after finding a seaside home for him and Ron to spend the summer in, it was a hugely enjoyable – not to mention lucrative – residency at Great Yarmouth's 1,500-capacity Pavilion Theatre. There was also time to squeeze in a *Seaside Special* for the BBC, featuring a young Lenny Henry and, once again, Bobby Crush, which aired on 9 September 1978.

It had been an enjoyable summer for John and Ron, and after a short break it was time to film season 6 of the sitcom that had made him one of the nation's biggest stars. Filming began on 29 October 1978 with a slightly less manic turnaround in airing each episode, which would enjoy a seventeen-day gap before being screened.

Six episodes were recorded including a Boxing Day special. They featured a new character, Mr Tebbs, played by the excellent James Hayter. David Croft did not replace Mr Grainger's character with another actor following Arthur Brough's death.

And the show was gaining a cult following far from these shores, with Australia and the Netherlands reporting sizeable audiences following the adventures of Mr Humphries, Mr Lucas and Mrs Slocombe, while earning the cast further income with numerous repeat fees they were paid as a result.

The success with Dutch viewers led to a whistle-stop trip to Amsterdam for John to promote the show. Tony Hare had become close friends with John and Ron and remembers a trip to Amsterdam around this period when Mr Humphries fever had gripped the Dutch:

I'd moved into radio, and I'd see John and Ron every now and then – sometimes they'd come to me for a meal or sometimes I'd go to their place.

John was quite different from his Mr Humphries character – he had a lovely sense of humour, but he was quite a quiet man and very softly spoken with a twinkle in his eye and I loved him dearly, he was such a lovely guy.

At one dinner party at his house, I arrived with a Gannex raincoat and a trilby, which I favoured at the time, and John answered the door and said, 'Good evening inspector, the body is in the library.' I didn't wear that coat and hat much after that!

I remember his first visit to Amsterdam, a place I know like the back of my hand because I've being going since the 1960s. John was doing a TV promo for *Are You Being Served?* in Holland, where it had become hugely popular, and by coincidence, we were both going to be in Amsterdam at the same time.

He said that my knowledge might be handy, and that we should meet up and that I could show him around, which is exactly what we did.

We met in the city, and we were sitting outside a pavement café where the tramlines ran past and at one point, and because it was warm he didn't have a hat or glasses on – which he wore quite often – and because we were by the kerb, when the tram pulled up, somebody must have spotted John, alerted others and everyone started shouting 'Are you free?' to John. He waved and said, 'I'm free!', which they absolutely loved! The Dutch people loved him wherever he went, and he was really chuffed that he was so popular over there. The Dutch used subtitles on British and American TV shows, so they knew John's real voice. Sometimes we'd be in a restaurant, people would come over and want to speak to John and he was always happy to, but Ron would occasionally say, 'Could you please leave us alone?' I liked Ron, but he could be quite curt at times and didn't stand for any nonsense. He had a bit of an attitude about him when he needed to.

John's friendship with Wendy Richard was set in stone and the pair socialised regularly, with John becoming a confidante for his close friend, especially when she was allegedly suffering from domestic abuse at the hands of her then-husband. The show's production manager, Susan Belbin recalls, 'John got on really well with Wendy and Mollie, though he made it his business to get on with everyone because he was such a professional. But he was especially close to Wendy.'

A sell-out stage version was performed in Australia as *Are You Being Served?* showed no signs of diminishing in popularity, at home or overseas. The programme was hugely popular Down Under and would lead to a once in a lifetime opportunity for John a little further down the line.

Doremy Vernon was still enjoying her brief appearances on the show and had become a part of the *Are You Being Served?* family, spending time with John outside filming and having dinner and drinks with him and Ron at their home in Little Venice, while storing away backstage secrets and stories. She recalled:

Frank Thornton was so good, but he was a pain in the arse at times, in my opinion! I did all my scenes with Frank, and I remember when he was late back from an *Are You Being Served?* tour of Australia on one occasion and Jeremy Lloyd stood in for him at rehearsals.

Jeremy was very arrogant and posh, and he was nowhere near as good as Frank. Frank had a certain way and the whole cast were like a jigsaw, they really were. I watch some scenes back and there was one with Mollie which was lovely, because John is listening to her intently and observing her timing. He was like that – very sharp – and when they were together, it was like a fencing fight – they got on really well.

Mollie was famous, but I don't know that she wanted to be. Wendy wanted fame because she needed the work, but I'm not sure Trevor Bannister wanted fame. I went to see Trevor in panto a few years later, and I said to him that I thought he was very generous in the early episodes with John. They were almost always in a two-shot and Trevor was so good at feeding John so he could get a laugh, and I think that often goes unnoticed. I really admired Trevor, but I think he got overshadowed because John became the real star.

In the Sunday transmission, food wasn't very good at the BBC so Wendy would provide a meal for everyone, and John would provide the dessert and it would all be held in John's dressing room. Trevor would provide the biscuits or cakes. Mollie was always too busy having her hair coloured for the latest incarnation of Mrs Slocombe, which had been her real hair at the start and then wigs later on. Nicholas Smith, who played Mr Rumbold, wasn't well liked, and he wasn't invited. He was very pompous, and though he got his laughs, he just wasn't very warm.

Arguably the BBC's most successful sitcom of the 1970s was still going strong as the decade entered its final year and series 7 was commissioned with the majority of the cast still on board.

James Hayter's brief stint as Mr Tebbs was ended – bizarrely – by the UK's biggest cake manufacturers. Hayter had been the narrator of the television ads for a company that had become a British institution during the 1970s with his cultured, grandfatherly delivery of the line, 'Mr Kipling makes exceedingly good cakes' being key to the company's success and brand image throughout its heyday. The company – Rank Hovis McDougall – preferred exclusivity for their main advertising asset and were prepared to pay a premium to protect their image. They paid Hayter a significant bonus to withdraw from appearing in a second series, feeling that his part as Mr Tebbs might tarnish the image he'd created advertising Mr Kipling if he continued with the risqué humour of *Are You Being Served?*

It was an easy choice for Hayter, who had enjoyed his one season at Grace Brothers, but as Frank Thornton commented, 'Who can blame an actor in his seventies for accepting money for staying at home? I would jump at the chance!' He would be replaced by Alfie Bass, another actor with a long and successful career behind him, who would take on the new role of Mr Goldberg.

Filming would again start in the autumn of 1979 and another stellar year for John Inman would end, as he loved best, in panto with *Mother Goose* at the Nottingham's Theatre Royal.

Another hectic twelve months lay ahead for the now 44-year-old actor, who was at the peak of his powers. There were several interesting offers on the table that he, his agent Bill Roberton and Ron would consider, including one intriguing approach that would give him the opportunity of working overseas for the first time. There was also the possibility of another sitcom on ITV where he would again be the star name.

Negotiations and discussions would bubble away in the background as John prepared for his role as Lord Fancourt Babberley, 'Babbs', in the Brandon Thomas farce *Charley's Aunt*. The production would open in Guildford the following April before touring the country for two months and then taking up a three-month residency at the Adelphi Theatre in London.

It would allow his heterosexual character to cross-dress and become the main protagonist's aunt, with predictably hilarious results. Model Sallyann Webster was an understudy in *Charley's Aunt*, and she remembers the experience of working with John fondly. She recalled:

I was in *Charley's Aunt* with John in 1979. We started in Guildford, which had been opposite the Guildford School of Acting where I'd learned my trade. We were encouraged to go over to the Yvonne Arnaud Theatre and help out, make tea, help with sets, and generally get a feel for the acting world, so that's how I ended up being part of the company.

After Guildford we toured and then did a ten-week run in London. It was a lovely production and a great opportunity for me to learn the ropes. I was an understudy for Belinda Carroll and Wendy Padbury, who was married to Melvyn Hayes at the time, and both ladies weren't very much older than me.

We had a very nice run with it, and I had the joy of doing everything – backstage assistant stage manager, dead body – you name it, I did it – as well as sorting out props and goodness knows what else for virtually no money!

I met John for the first time in rehearsals and he was utterly charming. I had to help him change costumes with a wardrobe guy called Streaky, who was lovely but completely mad in a fun sort of way! I think he was actually a close friend of John's.

Ron was incredibly protective, but I think we won him over eventually. John was adorable and polite and once you'd gained his respect, it remained. It was a lovely job to do because the cast were fabulous. I remember John and Ron were often dressed in black – I don't know why!

He was very inventive and if there were any bumps in the show, he'd pick it up and run with it – he was very professional and innovative.

Mark Wynter, who was cast as Jack Chesney, added that John was 'brilliant and so inventive'.

Long-time friends Peter Richards and Christine Ozanne went along to see John in the show – tickets for friends and family were never a problem – but Ozanne felt slightly differently to the actors he'd worked with in the production. She said: 'We remember seeing John in *Charley's Aunt* and thinking he wasn't as good as he usually was. His character, which is mainly quite butch, was all the funnier being in women's clothes later in the show, so John's persona may not have fitted the bill for the whole performance.'

Charley's Aunt did John's ever-increasing fame at home and abroad no trouble at all but on the day the run ended, filming of the seventh season of *Are You Being Served?* began. The latest batch of eight recordings would take up the next two months of his diary and include a panto-style Christmas special with the cast playing various characters and villains in a bid to win favour with the rest of the Grace Brothers' staff following a strike. John, dressed in a comical sailor's outfit, directs the show, bursting into tears with frustration several times as his colleagues fluff their lines or fool around.

'The Punch and Judy Affair' would also be – after forty-seven episodes and one movie – the last appearance for Trevor Bannister as Mr Lucas. The actor that *Are You Being Served?* had been reportedly sold to as a vehicle to continue his upward trajectory was seemingly now expendable, with the producers unwilling to change filming schedules for season 8 to accommodate him.

In many ways, Bannister's departure was a sad loss to the show, with his nervous energy, barbed comments and randy antics making Mr Lucas a huge part of its success, and it undoubtedly left a bad taste in his mouth. A popular member among the rest of the cast, he was the second key character the show lost. Alfie Bass, like James Hayter before him, would also leave after one season and Penny Irving – young Mr Grace's secretary – also departed after a twenty-one-episode run as Miss Bakewell.

There was little time for John to take a holiday or enjoy a break at home with Ron just yet, with his relentless schedule including another stint as *Mother Goose* at the New Theatre in Oxford. It was this sell-out show that would take him into a new decade and – incredibly, given what had come before – his busiest year yet.

9

Opportunity Knocks

As *Not the Nine O'Clock News* introduced UK audiences to a new, edgy and very youthful brand of alternative comedy, tried and tested sitcoms like *Are You Being Served?* were, in some people's eyes, starting to look a little dated. Just as crooners like Matt Monro had seen a seismic shift in what people were listening to and what the youth were demanding in the late 1960s, so the cast of Grace Brothers must have been looking nervously at what Rowan Atkinson, Mel Smith, Pamela Stephenson and Griff Rhys Jones were doing on their manic, smash-hit sketch show.

Nonetheless, an eighth season had been commissioned of *Are You Being Served?* and while a vibrant new breed of sitcom and sketch shows were quickly gaining sizeable audiences with a more punk rock element to their often anarchic humour, there was clearly still a place for the sitcom that had dominated the 1970s.

It must have also been an uncertain time for John Inman, with the camp Mr Humphries soon to be challenged by controversial and openly gay comedians like Julian Clary, whose suggestive and often outrageous act would see him wearing flamboyant clothing, sometimes PVC and bondage gear and flirting with straight men in the audience. This was a different kind of camp, and a very much 'in your face' attempt to stir the waters.

John was the subject of a number of articles around the time in which his portrayal of the 'mincing mother's boy from menswear' was interpreted by many as being a homosexual stereotype that an active and aggressive faction of the gay community were keen to move away from. For instance, in *The Face*, journalist Jon Savage, a high-brow commentator of popular culture of the day, having made his name covering punk rock and new wave for *NME* and *Melody Maker*, spoke of David Bowie and his transition from one look and persona to another. He wrote:

> If he wanted to avoid becoming a sharper, futuristic John Inman, Bowie had to move fast. He was already outgrowing Glam and its restrictions, while the public was celebrating Slade and Sweet – brickies dressed up as rent boys. It'd been good to him: the homosex angle had provided the scandal on which any sound teen career is based and glam had handed him a generation on a plate. Increasingly he pushed at the limits, offering himself as Artist, a generalist adopting different roles over a series of brilliant, yet reactive and reflexive albums.

How much John absorbed the talk around his characterisation of Mr Humphries is unclear, with his workload and demands on his time greater than ever. In fact, for a time, whatever was happening in the UK would largely have been immaterial to him as he flew out to Australia for what would be a five-month stint Down Under.

Due to the popularity of *Are You Being Served?*, Channel O had commissioned an Australian version of the sitcom with characters based on the British show, scripts based on episodes yet to be recorded in the UK and only one original cast member – John Inman – who reprised his role as Mr Humphries to an adoring Australian audience. Eight episodes were commissioned, written by David Croft and Jeremy Lloyd and with the director of the UK show, Bob Spiers, on board as well.

After Australia, John would tour the country in *Pyjama Tops* before returning home for an emotional final summer season in Blackpool – and then it would be off to panto at the Davenport Theatre in Stockport in what was an unrelenting schedule.

The Australian *Are You Being Served?* came at a cost to the British original – there simply wasn't time for him to squeeze in season 8, meaning for the first time in eight years there would be no new episodes for the BBC to air as an eighteen-month hiatus ensued because of John Inman's full-to-bursting diary.

The popular story behind Trevor Bannister's departure had been that he had committed to a lengthy tour of a play he was appearing in and therefore needed the filming of any new episodes to be filmed on a particular day of the week – something BBC executives weren't prepared to do. There were to be no concessions in his case, and he had been forced to leave as a result, but seemingly, there were concessions in John's case. This no doubt confirmed Bannister's suspicions that he'd become expendable.

Taking on the Mr Lucas role in the Australian version was relatively unknown comedian Shane Bourne. Now a successful TV host and celebrity in his homeland some forty-five years on, Bourne feels it was John who ensured he kept the role when the axe had been hovering above him. He recalls:

I auditioned for the show, as did everyone except June Bronhill and John Inman – June was a world-renowned opera singer with, as it turned out, quite a risqué sense of humour and this was to be her acting debut. I think John encouraged her, because although we had this warm-up guy, John used to do his own warm-up, which was pretty funny. June was up for a laugh and would drop the odd 'Shit!' in here and there, which nobody expected because of her persona.

In 1979, I was in a band, I was doing guest roles in cop shows – just anything that came up, really – and I'd done a bit of stand-up comedy in the early days, which was pretty unusual because there weren't a lot of comics around at that time and you'd end up working in strip clubs or in a footy club standing around a chair or trestle table, so I had some experience of comedy and the audition went well, I felt good about it, I got the role of Mr Randel and never looked back.

It felt great to be working with John, in particular. The UK version of *Are You Being Served?* was huge in Australia and there was a lot of British comedy on at the time – American comedies as well, but the British ones were right across the board. *Steptoe and Son* was huge and during my school years as a teenager, we grew up watching *The Two Ronnies*, Pete and Dud, *Monty Python* and all the sitcoms like *George and Mildred, Robin's Nest, Doctor in the House*, and I loved all that stuff!

It had a kind of bounce that you don't really see these days, so the opportunity for me to do something like this was fabulous.

As a matter of fact, I'd just done a British play called *The Comedians* by Trevor Griffiths, which is not about being funny, but more of a political statement set in mid-1970s Britain before the Thatcher years, and it was serious stuff. We were playing comedians with different styles, and there was one comedian who was very subversive and was trying to convey a political message, where there were others, like my character, who were just there to get laughs and take home the money.

So, when I got the role in *Are You Being Served?*, I was telling the actors in *The Comedians* about it and the reaction was, 'You're gonna do *that*?' from some of the more serious members of the fraternity, but it didn't bother me because I wasn't fully fledged in that culture, and I was doing all sorts of things and I'm really glad I did it because it was such fun. The multi-cam, live audience with masterful comedy people like John and the rest of the cast, it was a marvellous experience.

Knowing John was going to be in it was a huge incentive and the big carrot. When we were rehearsing, the British director Bob Spiers came out and he'd worked on *Dad's Army, Are You*

Being Served?, and *Fawlty Towers* and he was pleasantly surprised at the set-up, although in the early days, we actually rehearsed before John came out to Australia. We had a writer called Gene Burnett, who I'd worked with before and he had done a lot of variety stuff.

We were using pretty much the scripts from the UK – from the later series, maybe, which hadn't been aired yet – Gene might have just been making copies of the UK scripts. There was a bit of confusion because everyone was bunging on British accents and I was thinking, 'Isn't John coming to work in a department store out here in Australia?' so I didn't bother with the accent and some people felt that was remiss of me. After the first week of rehearsals, one of the producers took me to one side and said, 'Are you OK?' I said I was fine and enjoying myself and he said, 'You're not depressed are you?' I said, 'No, but I might be after this meeting!'

The guy who was the producer, Lyle McCabe was a cowboy – they all were – and we used to get paid in cash after each show. That was unusual even back then, but at least it was in an envelope! I got tired of hearing the line 'We'll see what happens when John gets here,' and they also warned me that they might have to let me go.

When John finally arrived, we did a run though and he was effusive towards me, which was fabulous because it shut those buggers up! I'm not sure what they wanted – maybe because I wasn't doing a Pommy accent, but John thought it was great. We got on like a house on fire, he was so knowledgeable because of his music hall, panto, and variety days and all the work he'd done. He was a master of the prop and was always sharing tips and advice. He'd say, 'Pick up the shirt with your right hand, because that means when you get over there, you'll be able to do this or that.' He was sort of choreographing everything and he'd been a dancer, and I think dancers who became actors were usually very meticulous, very disciplined, and usually very good at what they're doing – and

John was like that. There were a lot of laughs going on because his character was all so over the top, but everyone loved John – they just adored him.

Christine Amor took on Wendy Richard's Miss Brahms role, though under the name Miss Nicholls, and was the junior assistant to June Bronhill's Mrs Crawford (Mrs Slocombe). Now a veteran star of Australian film and television, she remembers working with John Inman well:

The first time I became aware of John Inman was watching the English version of *Are You Being Served?*.

He was definitely a star of the show and I auditioned for the role of Miss Nicholls with the director Bob Spiers after my agent had put me forward and secured it almost immediately.

I first met John at the opening day of rehearsals in the Melbourne city rehearsal rooms. I loved his flamboyant nature, but I was a little in awe of him, so we didn't get super close.

I remember going out with him to a Chinese restaurant in the city and his horror at seeing the chicken feet that we ordered. Also, his assessment that compared to London the only thing really to do in Melbourne he would say is to 'f***' – always a wicked twinkle in his eye.

He was great fun and he loved being here – I think he also respected working with Bob Spiers, who later went on to direct the *Ab Fab* series. I met Ron, who was often in the rehearsal room, where he always kept a respectful low profile.

For me, the series was great fun, especially working with a live audience, and even though we would at times do several takes, they would respond and laugh as if they had only heard the dialogue for the first time – just delightful. John was a master at keeping the audience entertained and happy.

Also adapting the series to the Australian vernacular was at times interesting as we needed to capture our particular Australian style of humour within the given text. John was always the motor and lead, and we followed his style as best we could – after all he was the master.

Shane Bourne continued:

We filmed for ATV-O on Channel O, which later became Channel 10, in Melbourne out in Nunawading, some forty-five minutes out of town, and I'd worked there a few times before. There was nothing in Nunawading, and you kind of had the place to yourself, but we'd only shoot out there and rehearse elsewhere. We'd have a camera rehearsal and then we'd shoot the episode the next day and it was a pretty well-oiled machine. But thank god for John because he was almost co-directing and writing at the same time, and when I look back, it was a nice opportunity for John and Ron to come out here, and I think they loved it.

We'd film one a week and the whole time period for a series would be about ten weeks. The beauty of that was we would rehearse for four days, get the weekend off, a day for camera rehearsals and then a day for recording. Often, they'd play the previous week's recording to get the audience warmed up, not only to get the vibe, but to record the laughter as well.

It had a very theatrical feel to it with all the counters – the men's and the women's department and the stairs coming down from the lifts, it was a great idea. If we were rehearsing in the city, we'd go over the road for a drink or maybe have a Chinese meal afterwards and it was all very relaxed. If June had one G&T too many, she could get a bit savage – she was hilarious, larger than life and great fun.

I think John and Ron were staying just outside of the city and we were all invited over, and they put on a bit of a do, which was all very relaxed. John and I shared a number of scenes that were very funny. I remember being in the office in one scene and John was crying and I had to interpret what he was saying, and it was pure vaudeville music hall entertainment. Because my dad had been an entertainer and had been exposed to all that style and entertainers, I had a real appreciation of it all. It was a gift.

I wasn't chased down the street or anything, but if we were out with John, it was a different story – they couldn't believe it. They were pretty knocked out about it. Australians had a sense of isolation and a cultural cringe to a certain extent. He'd stop and chat whenever anyone recognised him, was very personable and then move on before he got trapped – there was an art in that. As much as he was an over the top, camp character and outrageous, I never thought of his character as gay. It wasn't to do with sexual preferences, it was more about lifestyle and John personified all that. That was half the fun of being in the acting industry – it wasn't 9 to 5, and it was quite rebellious in many ways.

I can't tell you just how much I learned working with John, but his timing was almost scientific. I read that originally Mr Humphries was just one of many characters and Trevor Bannister was meant to be the focus as a sort of everyman caught up in this weird world of a department store, but eventually John and Mollie became the huge stars and ran away with the money.

Ron was introduced as his personal assistant and that's what he was – he looked after John in a professional way. I recall Bob Spiers saying that he'd thought it would have been a bit 'How's your father?' working in the land Down Under but that he thought the crew, cast and everyone involved had been superb. There was a vibe and a kind of optimism that made it all wonderful and having John and June involved made it all come together and gave it a theatrical feel. They were great days.

He was very supportive to me. He used to say, 'If we were in the UK, Shane would be a massive star,' because Trevor Bannister was and the British still celebrate their stars and celebrities, whereas in Australia for many years, if their performers started being too successful, they'd want to cut them down to size. Not so much now. So an element of self-depreciation was needed, and that's a sort of British thing as well. In America, that's completely different and unless you sell yourself and be your own promoter, they don't want to know and will quickly move on.

Because John was at the helm, Bob was directing, and we had good scripts written by David Croft and Jeremy Lloyd; it all just had a really good feel to it. It was a great night out for the audiences who watched it. It was a terrific time for me, and I look back on it with only warm feelings.

With season 1 of the Aussie *Are You Being Served?* in the can, John took a short holiday before the second part of his adventure Down Under continued with the tour of *Pyjama Tops*. It was all aboard the Inman Express, next stop New South Wales ...

10

Troubled Waters?

Almost every relationship has its ups and downs, and John Inman and Ron Lynch's was no different.

Close friends had previously suggested Ron could be controlling at times and possessive towards John, isolating people he had known for many years. However, if he was taking the role of manager seriously, it could also be true that he was managing John's ever-increasing workload and ensuring there were periods when he could rest. John never liked to say no to anything, so it made sense to have someone around who would when the occasion demanded. However, there were moments during the 1980 trip to Australia that suggested things might have been difficult between the couple on occasion.

Actor and playwright Barry Creyton had been cast to appear in *Pyjama Tops*, which began a seven-week tour of the country on 14 April at Newcastle in New South Wales. A week later, the play would move to the Theatre Royal in Sydney for three weeks, before spending another three weeks at Her Majesty's in Melbourne and finally a week at Hobart at the start of June.

Creyton witnessed what he called 'destructive behaviour' at times by Ron, who enjoyed his drink and, like John, was also a heavy smoker. Creyton, who now lives and works in the USA, recalled:

I was aware of Ron's drinking but never of John's. John was always meticulous in performance and his theatre behaviour was never less than professional. He was a joy to work with. Even though he was, by the nature of the piece, the centre of attention, he never pulled focus from another actor, never upstaged, allowed every cast member their moment.

I always wonder about destructive relationships and have written quite a bit of fiction about them. There were many dressing room outpourings about Ron's treatment of him, sometimes bringing him near to tears, but he always went back for more.

I tend to think both parties in such a relationship tend to enjoy the drama to a degree. As I said, I was always a sympathetic ear, but never offered advice. I remember one thing he said in one of our pre-show confabs. He related some argument he'd had with Ron that day and added emotionally, 'It's like broken biscuits in my brain.' He wondered how he could go on and play a comedy that night. But of course, he did with not a laugh lost.

Perhaps the pressures of being overseas and in each other's back pockets continually for several months was talking its toll – that plus the searing heat. In Australia, they had very few friends to socialise with and there were few opportunities to go off and do their own thing whenever they pleased as they could in London. If anything, it seems the issues were likely nothing more than a form of cabin fever.

Creyton enjoyed the experience of *Pyjama Tops* immensely:

In 1980, my name was known nationally on stage and TV. The British director of *Pyjama Tops* contacted my agent and asked if I'd be interested in taking on the leading man to John's character lead in the play. I was playing a recurring guest star role in a TV series at the time, and my agent, cognisant of the workload, declined on my behalf. However, the request reached me personally and I immediately accepted. I juggled schedules for both rehearsals and performance in Sydney.

Of course, I knew of John from the years I worked in London and due to the Australian success of the British *Are You Being Served?* I met him for the first time when rehearsals began, and we established a warm working relationship from the start. I also had a great relationship with the director, who appreciated and encouraged the stage rapport John and I had.

I rode motorcycles in those days and John frequently referred to me as 'the Bikie'. But it was an invaluable means of rapid transport from the TV studio to the downtown Sydney Theatre Royal on days I was shooting late.

As I say, John's partner was with him in Sydney, and they were going through rough times. John often came to my dressing room before the curtain to give me the day's woes, but never asked advice – mercifully. In those days, relationships were not my area of expertise, but as I say, I always offered a sympathetic ear.

Johnny Lockwood, who was a well-known comedy man in London as well as in Australia, was also in the cast. For some reason he latched onto John as a fellow Brit comedian and often inundated him with anecdotes. This gave John another reason to spend the half hour before curtain up in my dressing room – to avoid Johnny Lockwood! Johnny would put his head into to my dressing room to ask if I'd seen John. 'No,' I was obliged to lie, while John hid behind a rack of costumes! Life imitating farce!

Playing on stage with John was wonderful. His timing was impeccable and we neither of us trod on the other's laughs. One of the cast was an actress who was a known quantity on TV but had had little stage experience. On more than a few occasions, she spoke lines during prolonged audience laughter and John urged her to consider her timing. She came to me and asked, 'What *is* timing?'

My reply reduced John to belly laughs, which he hurried off to conceal. My terse advice: 'It's simple. If they laugh, don't talk. If they don't laugh, talk.'

As for the Australian audiences? They loved him. And he, naturally enough, loved being loved by them! By the time the Melbourne season came up, I was done with my guest stint on the

TV series so went with the play, which was also an enormous success. Channel 10 proposed a TV special for John while he was in the country which featured songs and sketches and several guest stars, of which I was one.

Shane Bourne was another invited guest on the special, and he recalls that the station pulled out all the stops for their guest star:

John did a one-hour special for that network while he was here, and it was a real traditional variety show. He arrived in a pink helicopter and landed on the studio helipad with top hat and tails in front of a curtain and he'd chat to the audience and the viewers at home, burst through the door and do a huge dance number and then we'd do sketches. People would come out in their droves to see him because there wasn't a lot of stuff like that going on in Australia at that time and they loved the whole experience.

Barry Creyton recalls one musical sketch he'll never forget:

The routine we did was based on one he performed often in the UK. I was announced as being a major exponent of ballroom dancing accompanied by my lovely partner Joylene. I entered in white tie and tails and announced apologetically that Joylene was held up in traffic. John complained that he'd already hired the orchestra, so we had to make the best of it. And he, in dinner jacket, did the routine with me. We did foxtrot, waltz, polka, jive, rock'n'roll — me with a deadpan face while John got into the spirit of it with extra flourishes and much batting of the eyelashes.

I loved doing this routine with him — but it wasn't without pain. My dancing skills have never progressed beyond an amiable soft shoe. I rehearsed for two weeks with the choreographer for that routine. Once in a while during that tour, John and I and Ron would get together for supper, but the black cloud hanging over their relationship during that period defeated me ultimately, and I sometimes pleaded fatigue.

I worked in the UK from the late 1960s to the late '70s and John and I had many mutual friends, but even though I returned for brief visits in the '80s, I never saw him again. Often we'd exchange greetings via the mutuals.

There were dates in New Zealand as well that also played to packed out houses, and it was here that John bumped into another huge star of the BBC, Dick Emery, who was on tour with his own solo show.

Emery and his girlfriend Fay Hillier, who had appeared on *The Benny Hill Show*, *Dick Emery's Comedy Hour* and *Blake's 7*, recalls how they first spotted John – and what happened next:

The very first time John and I met was in 1982 New Zealand where I was staying with Dick Emery. He was in *Pyjama Tops* at the time, and we were staying at the same hotel when we arrived, we saw John stretched out by the pool. I'd never met him before, but obviously Dick had, so he asked to borrow my high heels and then tottered over towards him. John turned around and looked extremely cross because he must have thought this old queen was coming over to speak to him, but then he realised it was Dick, they embraced and laughed, and we ended up going for drinks later that evening.

I got to know him a tiny bit at that point, but not that much, but John and Dick were both touring New Zealand and Australia, and later, when we were in Perth, John was playing somewhere nearby. Dick was ill one night and couldn't go on stage so we tried to find out if John could possibly step in, so we didn't have to send the audience home, but it wasn't possible for one reason or another. Dick didn't get any better and we had to close the show and go back to London.

After five months of hard work, searing heat and relationship squabbles, John and Ron also headed back to London. Professionally, it had been a wonderfully successful trip, with Australian audiences lapping up John's performances. He'd stepped outside his comfort zone – albeit into a play he knew inside out as well as being in a version of the sitcom that had made him a star – and he returned to the UK ready to go again.

For a third time, John would perform a summer season of his show *Fancy Free*, with a three-month run in his hometown of Blackpool. The famous ABC Theatre would host the show, a 1,934-capacity venue that had hosted the Beatles, Cilla Black, Tommy Steele and Morecambe and Wise over the years and had a revolving stage.

However, John's residency would be the ABC's and Blackpool's last major summer season variety show with times and audience demands changing. The theatre's future lay in a different kind of entertainment after *Fancy Free*, which would run from 4 July to 4 October 1980, as it was converted into a cinema. Bobby Crush was once again on board, and the show was another roaring success.

The stresses and strains of the Australian tour seem to have been blown away by the blustery winds off the Irish Sea and allowed John to see his mum regularly as well as his nieces and extended family and friends. And how fitting that one of Blackpool's favourite sons should be in the last summer show at the iconic ABC? Although there would be the occasional live act up until December, John's variety act was the last big deal before its revamp.

Mother Goose alongside *Coronation Street*'s Lynne Perrie at Stockport's Davenport Theatre brought 1980 to a successful close, and John was informed that the Australian version of *Are You Being Served?* had done well enough in the ratings to warrant a second series. So 1981 was already looking an equally if not even busier year for the tireless entertainer, who also now had a sizeable official fan club run by his 'secretary', Carole Browne.

11

Back to ITV

It had been a long time coming, but Barry Howard finally had the national audience he had craved after winning a part in David Croft and Jimmy Perry's new comedy *Hi-De-Hi!*. Howard would play one half of the upper-class dance instructors, Yvonne and Barry Stuart-Hargreaves. If there had been any professional jealousy or tension in his friendship with John Inman, there was an opportunity to rekindle what had been a long and successful partnership now they were on a more equal footing.

That would be, of course, if and when John had a gap in his itinerary, which looked unlikely, as filming for the second Australian series of *Are You Being Served?* was wrapped up with a shorter stay Down Under for the eight episodes filmed. John was in danger of a Mr Humphries overload as filming for season eight of the BBC's *Are You Being Served?* began in early April 1981.

The characters of Young Mr Grace, Mr Goldberg and Mr Lucas had all left the show, and filling in the sizeable footsteps of Trevor Bannister's similar role was musician and actor Mike Berry, who had a couple of Top 10 hits under his belt as well as being a staple cast member of the hit 1970s series *Worzel Gummidge*. Berry said:

I got the role because Trevor Bannister wasn't available, and my agent Richard Stone was called by David Croft, who asked if he had anybody that might be suitable for the part. Fortunately, he said, 'Yes, I've got the very man' – I'd only been with him a month! I went into read for David and Jeremy Lloyd and I got the part.

I'd just had a Top 10 hit and had ten years of commercials behind me as well, so that helped. I was the king of commercials back then, along with Max Mason – I don't know why – but if Max or I was ever up for a commercial, the other actors auditioning would groan because our faces just seemed to fit.

The part of Mr Spooner came along as something extra because I was doing singing and acting, and I'd been in *Worzel Gummidge* with Jon Pertwee. I'd never met John Inman previous to *Are You Being Served?*, but he was very nice, and a joy to be around and we got along very well. We used to go to the pub at lunchtime during rehearsals along with Wendy Richard and he was just funny. He used to take the Mickey out of people but in a nice, gentle way and find funny things about them.

He always had some great stories to tell, he was happy, and he just enjoyed life. He liked partying, being with his partner Ron and having a good time. John and Mollie got all the big laughs, of course – they were a couple of old pros who worked it out between them because the series was twelve years of bliss, really.

David Croft and Jeremy Lloyd had the final say, but they were always open to cast suggestions if they worked well and they didn't mind where they came from because we had seasoned actors like Arthur English, and they liked their input. There was one occasion when Mollie had a perfume set on her counter and Arthur came on set, passed the counter, and sniffed the air and then looked at the bottom of his shoe as though he'd stepped in dogshit – it wasn't in the script, but David Croft loved it and said, 'We're keeping that in!' – and that's how it was.

I remember David coming up to me at my first run through and he just said, 'That's perfect, keep it like that.' But I'd just been playing myself, really – a bit more downmarket maybe and a bit more Cockney. I'd lived among Cockneys all my life, even though my parents were a bit posher, so I was familiar with the sort of character I wanted to play. I had a middle-London accent, I suppose, that I used to crank up to full-on Cockney at school and then I'd tone it back down when I got home. I'm still like that now depending on who I'm talking to!

John was always very nice to me, and I remember Wendy Richard saying, 'You'll be alright, you've got John's seal of approval.' That amounted to John saying to her, 'He can do it,' after our first rehearsal. He didn't want anyone who was too wooden because we did have some actors come on the show who weren't very good – they'd try too hard, or they just didn't have that something you need.

The humour was so blunt and easy to see, it cut through a lot of barriers – it was slapstick and a bit like a saucy seaside postcard. It became John and Mollie's show in many ways. It was one episode per week. We'd go in for a read through on a Monday and knock off early. Tuesday, Wednesday, and Thursday we'd rehearse and Friday we'd record.

The rehearsal room was like a big gym with boxes and barriers indicating where the set props would be with tape markings for camera angles. So five days from start to finish for each episode over eight weeks. Because I joined eight seasons in, it was a well-oiled machine.

Obviously Trevor Bannister couldn't do the eighth season because he had commitments elsewhere, but the cast were very wary but warm and welcoming. Frank Thornton was old school and a bit more guarded, but they just didn't want any dickhead coming in and walking all over their laughs. That's why John's seal of approval was so important.

I'd say John was probably closest to Wendy. They used to go drinking together and she'd have a bottle of champagne a day. There would be an ice bucket with a bottle of champagne on ice waiting for her in the Volunteer in Baker Street, where she frequented each day because she lived nearby. As soon as she walked in from rehearsals, that bottle of bubbly would be there.

I don't think Wendy was that happy and her husband was a drinker. She looked at me in a longing way once, but I was married with two kids and not interested at all. She said to me one day, 'Wanna come in my dressing room and look at the ceiling?' I thought, oh yeah, I think I'll pass. That said, she was saying it a jokey way.

I didn't socialise much outside of filming because we all had our own private lives, and I don't think any of us had the same interests. John was always good to me and never told me to say a line in a certain way because he was an old-time pro.

It was over the top and camp at times, but that's why the public loved it and later, so did the Americans in years to come. I felt privileged to have known and worked with John on such a wonderful show.

With season 8 in the can – including a Christmas Eve special – it was time for John to start focusing on his new ITV sitcom, *Take a Letter Mr Jones*.

With an impressive cast that included Rula Lenska, Miriam Margolyes and old friend Christine Ozanne, it was something new and interesting for John, who, in a refreshing role reversal, would play the male secretary to his female boss (Rula Lenska). It was undoubtedly better than his previous ITV outing, the lamentable *Odd Man Out*, and was written by the 'two Ronnies' (Ronald Chesney and Ronald Wolfe), who had enjoyed so much success with their *On the Buses* series and movie spin-offs.

Filmed on the south coast and produced by Southern Television, a series of six episodes was filmed for airing in September. It was a show that Rula, Miriam and Christine enjoyed immensely. Rula remembered:

We had wonderful times together, not just working but as a friendship. John and Ron's flat in Maida Vale was occasionally an open house and Miriam Margolyes would sometimes be there when he had these sort of soirees where he'd invite a group of people around with drinks and nibbles and we'd tell stories and, of course, John was paramount at that – many of them incredibly rude, incredibly vulgar, and incredibly funny!

I remember when we were doing *Take a Letter Mr Jones*, Miriam was playing the nanny to my daughter and on the rehearsals floor, Miriam would come up with these outrageous stories – mostly sexual – and I'd have to put my hands around the ears of this small child so she couldn't hear.

I didn't know anyone in the cast at that point. In *Take a Letter Mr Jones*, which was a classic reversal with me being the boss and John being my secretary, it was a nice idea and I'm surprised it didn't go any further. I recall it being received quite well, but like a lot of things I've done over the years, *Rock Follies* in particular, it's never been repeated.

Much-loved actress, entertainer and best-selling author Miriam Margolyes also has only good memories of the time she worked on *Take a Letter Mr Jones*. Speaking from her winter home in Tuscany, she said:

It was a very happy company – John had the gift of making every-one happy. I don't remember that much about it because it was so long ago.

John used to regale us with his stories of the theatre because he was a vaudevillian, because he obviously wasn't just a TV star and his way with an audience was stunning – he was terrific, and he just loved performing and loved to laugh and I loved him, and he was a darling. It was a very happy programme to be involved in.

He was still in *Are You Being Served?* at the time, which had made him a household name, but I'd never worked with him before. He was just a sweetheart. I've always been an 'out' lesbian and talked about that without any inhibition, but John came from a time when that was not acceptable and while he was obviously gay, I don't know how much the public knew for sure.

There was Larry Grayson, Frankie Howerd and Kenneth Williams around at the time, whereas Wilfrid Brambell was totally in the closet, but I don't know of many other gay actors of that era who were open about their sexuality and John was always very careful in that area. He wasn't exactly in the closet, but he didn't put it about much. He had his partner Ron, of course, but he was somewhat guarded, I suppose.

For Christine Ozanne, it was happy reunion with her friend of twenty years. She recalled:

Take a Letter Mr Jones was wonderful and John was absolutely marvellous. He was the glue who held everything together and diplomatically sort any issues out on behalf of others.

I think I was offered the part and I'm certain John had something to do with that. I don't recall going to meet producer Brian Izzard, but I'd worked with him before. We recorded it in Southampton for Southern Television.

On one occasion, we'd finished filming in mid-July, and it just happened to be the day before my birthday and we were all going for a meal afterwards, but it was getting later and later and I said, 'If we're here for much longer, I'll be having my birthday right here.' Miriam then said, 'Oh Christine – is it your birthday?' as if she didn't know, just as this cake with candles arrived that John had arranged.

I think it was to do with John and his agent that we only did one season. I think John had enjoyed so much success with *Are You Being Served?* and I think his agent wanted to squeeze as much out of that as he could, so although John really liked making the show with us, I think his agent was the main reason there wasn't a second series. They probably thought it wasn't going to take off.

John would remain friends with Rula, Miriam and Christine for the remainder of his life, but with filming for *Take a Letter Mr Jones*

complete, there were a number of engagements to fulfil for the rest
of the year.

Although viewing figures for *Are You Being Served?* were starting to decline, BBC executives thought it was certainly worthy of
a ninth season, though the gap between filming season 8 and season
9 was the most yet – twenty months in total – freeing up much of
1982 for John. He also wasn't too disappointed the Australian version of the show had not got a third series, feeling he had extensively
explored a new opportunity and more than enjoyed his stay in the
country, where he planned to return in future years. In his eyes, it
had been an adventure that had run its course.

Shane Bourne felt the show could have maybe gone again, but the
plans had been poorly executed:

I don't think it occurred to anyone to distribute it overseas – we
weren't even sure who had the rights when you're being paid
in cash!

It was like coal to Newcastle as far as selling it to the UK and it
was probably seen as Australians doing British comedy, so I could
understand it in some ways.

It rated well enough to go to a second series and it was well-
received – was it enough to go to a third series? I'm not sure, but
I'm also not sure that was the issue. John had come out and filmed
two series and done his time in Australia and had other things to
pursue. I think we'd have been asking for trouble if we were just
churning out what had already been a huge success in the UK and
around the world. Comedy is an area of writing that's been over-
looked in Australia, big time, whereas in the UK and America it's
in the DNA.

It felt like the Grace Brothers adventure was slowly coming to a natural conclusion, though the remaining cast members – all of whom
had become household names on the back of the series – were keen
to continue for the time being. David Croft would not be co-writ-
ing the ninth series, although he would take on an advisory role and

would attend the final read throughs. It wasn't quite the end of an era, but *Are You Being Served?*, like everything else on TV, had a shelf life and one, perhaps two, more seasons at best, seemed to be likely at that stage.

12

Less is More

John Inman's ITV experiment seemed to be over. Though *Take a Letter Mr Jones* had been a modest success and held its own in the ratings, a second season wasn't commissioned and followed *Odd Man Out* into the file marked 'one-series wonders'. Screened in the autumn of 1981, the cast was strong, and the premise was decent, but it lacked the sparkle and wit that John was capable of bringing to the table with the right scriptwriters.

His reputation was still intact, and he was still very much in demand, appearing at the 1981 Royal Variety Performance at London's Theatre Royal in late November. As always, the public had plenty of time for John Inman.

In the royal show, he appears in character as Mr Humphries and discovers his next customer is former British boxing champion Henry Cooper, who he proceeds to start measuring up for a new suit.

'Ere, what's your game?' says Cooper as John reaches around his waist with the tape.

Mr Humphries then says, 'Now for the bit you're dreading, and the bit they can't wait for. I'm going to measure your inside leg.'

As he's about to attempt exactly that, the bell rings, Cooper claims he's been 'saved by the bell' and John starts a short song and gentle dance routine alongside the boxer, dressing Cooper with a new jacket, hat and carnation before both take the warm applause of the audience, bow before the Queen and exit stage left.

Christmas and New Year would be ushered in – for the sixth year in succession – with the *Mother Goose* panto at Victoria Palace, London, which meant John could return home after each performance instead of there being a monotonous month-long hotel stay.

With no television series to film in 1982, a decade of being a regular fixture in the living rooms up and down the land had been paused temporarily and John was free to enjoy the riches of his work and take a well-earned break. He would return to the stage for a three-month run in *My Fat Friend* later in the year, but he was able to enjoy his forty-seventh year largely at home with Ron and spending time entertaining friends.

Ironically, in his absence, Barry Howard's *Hi-De-Hi!* was going strong and attracting excellent viewing figures, while the anarchic alternative sitcom *The Young Ones*, *The Comic Strip Presents*, *The Kenny Everett Television Show* and *Not the Nine O'Clock News* continued breaking new ground and squeezing some of the milder, more traditional sitcoms off the schedule altogether. John Lloyd, creator of *Not the Nine O'Clock News*, said that though there was a gaping chasm between traditional sitcoms and alternative comedy, the writing team had a healthy respect for *Are You Being Served?* and the craft of David Croft and Jeremy Lloyd:

Like anything else on telly, 1970s sitcoms were of uneven quality. We had a little pop at them in a sketch on *Not the Nine O'Clock News*, mentioning shows like *Terry and June*, *Life Begins at 40*, *Robin's Nest* and *Rings on their Fingers*.

But there were many great sitcoms, too, and I don't remember anyone wanting to target *Are You Being Served?* They had a great cast of characters – John Inman very much included – and were masterfully co-written and produced by David Croft.

Like *Monty Python*, *Not the Nine O'Clock News* spent quite a lot of time parodying other TV shows, such as *That's Life* and *Stout Life*, which was a parody of LWT's *Gay Life* – and much more, too, but *Are You Being Seved?* was not among them, which is quite a compliment in a strange way ...

There was an ongoing battle of sorts going on between old and new, with Benny Hill, Les Dawson and even Morecambe and Wise in one corner, and the likes of Ben Elton, Rowan Atkinson, Julian Clary and Alexei Sayle in the other – they were two worlds that couldn't have been further apart. Mother-in-law jokes and seaside sauciness was on the wane, politically sharp humour and hitting each other in the face with frying pans was on the up. A changing of the guard, in many respects, was under way.

Of course, John took it all in his stride.

He would meet regularly with Wendy Richard and Barbara Windsor – another Cockney girl who had become a huge star, thanks to her nine appearances in the *Carry On* series – and had a wide circle of friends who would enjoy lavish dinner parties at his home in Little Venice. Many memories, not to mention heavy hangovers, were created in his top-floor attic bar.

His main focus for the year was reprising his role as Henry in a production of *My Fat Friend*, a part he had briefly stood in for a week a decade earlier. The play would try out in Lincoln before embarking on a two-month residency at the Devonshire Park Theatre in Eastbourne. Patricia Brake would be the co-star in what was a 'four-hander' with Nicholas Field and Niall Gavin. Gavin recalls:

> We did a try out in Lincoln for a week before moving on to Eastbourne and as a struggling actor at the time, I really thought it might be the start of something for my career, but John was the main attraction obviously and I couldn't get any agents to come to Eastbourne to watch me, but it was a great, fun summer.
>
> John had done *My Fat Friend* before and knew it inside out and he was very helpful with the cast and the director in making it work. Given where I was at the time, it was the first time I'd worked with an actor of that calibre.

Patricia Brake was the co-star and she'd played Ronnie Barker's daughter in the *Porridge* spin-off *Going Straight*. They were the leads, Nicholas Field and myself were relative unknowns – it was a four-hander. I'd done just one rep season at Chesterfield at that time.

John and I got on really well. He was delightfully polite and unassuming. He wasn't starry at all but super professional. He was very generous with his time and advice. Bill Roberton was the director, and it was a remarkably easy play to get into. There was a lot of fun and laughter at rehearsals, and I was a little star-struck with it all. John was very encouraging, and I was fortunate because my character played a lot off John, and I was on stage for most of the play with either John or Patricia. I loved it and it was a great chance to see a recognised comedic actor up close and learn from him and Patricia, and it certainly upped my game. Bill knew how to get the best out of us.

After the play, John would go his own way, very quietly and without fuss. John was staying at the Grand Hotel with Ron and was clearly enjoying the fruits of his career. I was living in a flat in Shepherd's Bush in London, but every Saturday night when the show came down, John would go home to London until Tuesday morning. He had a driver waiting for him and Ron. John asked where I lived and when I told him, he said I could jump in their car and he'd drop me off on the way. I thought that was such a kind gesture and one that I took him up on. He did everything properly, too, and there was a bottle of wine waiting in the car and sandwiches and John and Ron shared those with me. It was an hour and a half to get home, and though I didn't travel back to Eastbourne with them, it saved me a bit of money. Ron was very quiet and was pitched to me as John's business partner, but it was clearly more than that. He just stayed in the background, really. He had John's back and was very unobtrusive. They were very affectionate together but not overly so. John was quiet and contemplative, and not like the character that made him famous on the small screen.

The local critics were effusive with their praise, as you'd expect because they were catering for a dedicated audience, and given the demographic, it was mainly made up of retirees; it felt like we had somebody collapse at every show for one reason or another. They were absolutely the right audience to lap up *My Fat Friend* with John and Patricia.

We chatted a lot and he never made me feel that I wasn't an equal – I asked how he coped with the fame and that he was the big draw for the play. He was very recognisable, so did he get pestered a lot?

He said, 'Of course – I can't go anywhere without people shouting, "I'm free!" I've been in the business for years and I got famous for forgetting a line very early in *Are You Being Served?*, so I made one up and just said "I'm free!" and that is what is paying for this car, the wine, the sandwiches and staying at the Grand, so if people recognise me and enjoy my performances then that fame and intrusion is a small price to pay for me being able to live the sort of life I do.'

I thought that was a lovely attitude to have. He accepted that being public property in some ways came with territory.

I never saw John again after *My Fat Friend* and I went on and worked for four or five more years before getting married and eventually coming out of acting all together. I loved working with him, and it gave me a taste of what it might have been like to work in the West End.

The year 1982 had undoubtedly been a gentler one for John and he ended it as he loved to end most years: in panto with *Mother Goose*, this time at the Empire Theatre in Liverpool with Dawson Chance and Barbara Newman.

Why shoot the goose that was laying golden eggs annually?

Childhood home: 18 Garden Street,
Preston, as it is today.

One of the many shows John did with
friend and mentor Sid James.

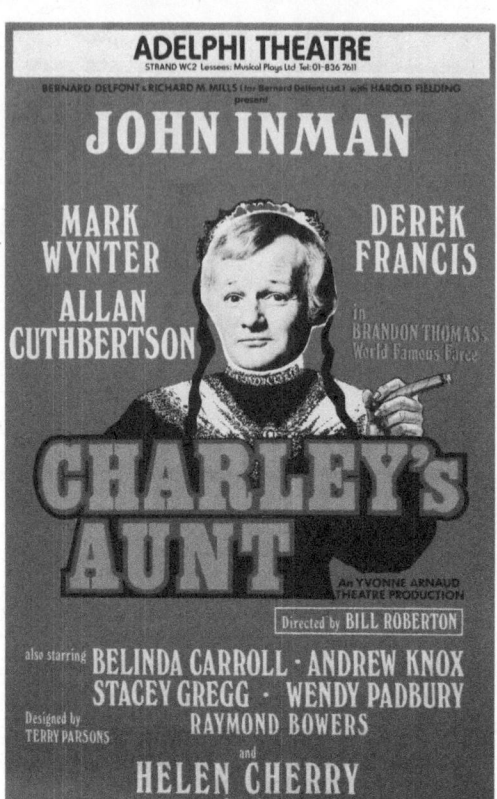

Charley's Aunt: a successful show for John that included cross-dressing!

Elaborate costumes, usually designed and created by John, were standard for panto season.

n the set of the 1977 film version of *Are You Being Served?* with Arthur Brough and Wendy Richard.

On set for a festive *Are You Being Served?* 'Happy Returns' was first aired on Boxing Day 1978.

A promotional BBC still of a festive gathering at Grace Brothers. (© BBC)

More promotion for the stage show, with John clearly having top billing in his home town!

John appears in a sketch on the hugely successful *Basil Brush Show*, October 1976. Boom, boom!

On of the many *Mother Goose* panto posters ...

On the set of *Are You Being Served?* Down Under style, with Shane Bourne (far left).

John: the life and soul of any party …

John with close friend Barbara Windsor at a London charity event.

Most of the *Are You Being Served?* cast take a publicity shot in Blackpool during their successful stage run in the town.

John in *Mother Goose* alongside Christopher Biggins – arguably the heir to John's panto dame throne.

With Wendy Richard in Blackpool – and the obligatory champagne!

John in his element on tour in Bedside Manners circa 1989.

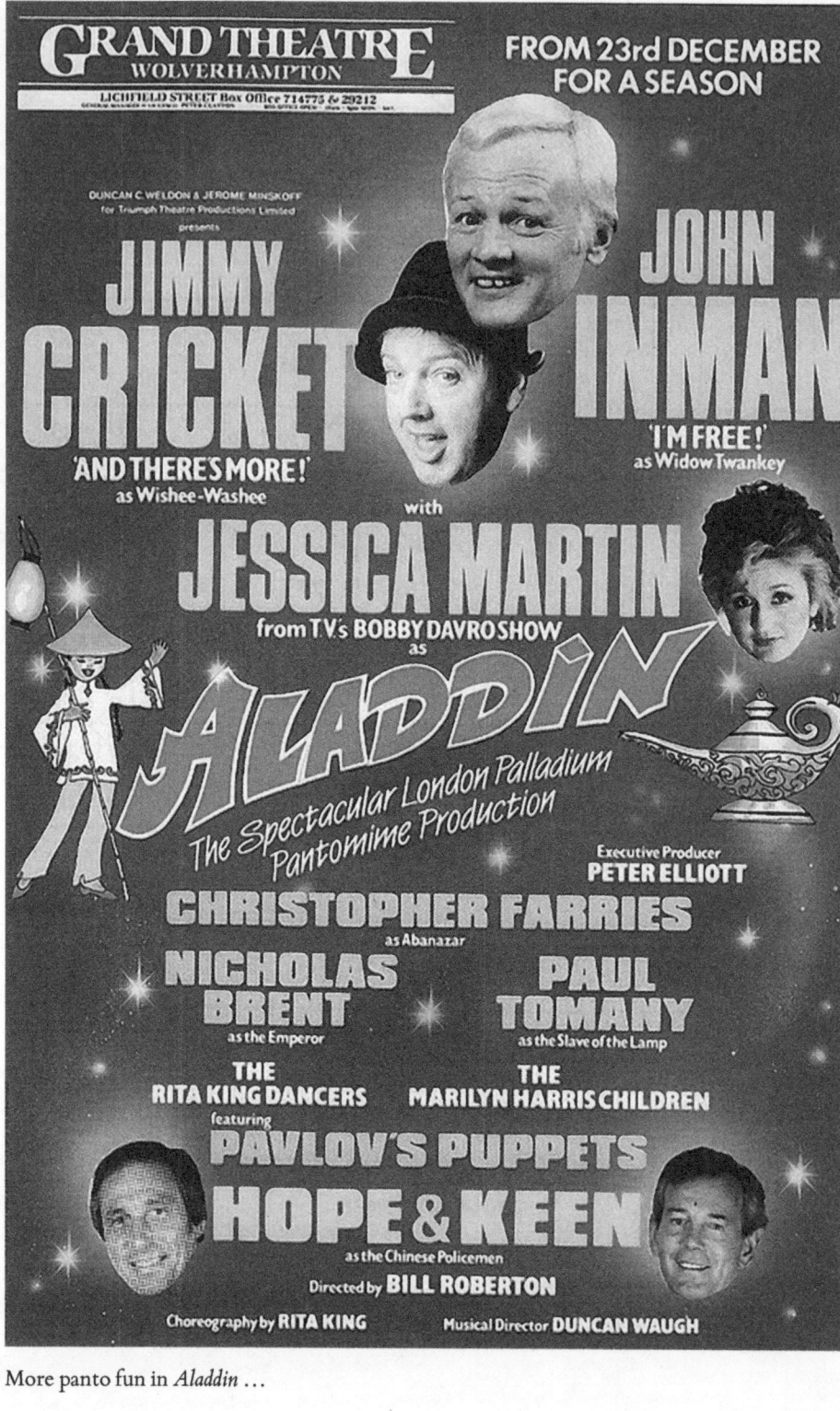

More panto fun in *Aladdin* …

ohn is faced with the formidable Diana Yardswick – played by the wonderful Doremy Vernon – during a role-reversal episode of *Are You Being Served?* called 'The Club' (season 6). (© Radio Times)

Filming for the US PBS channel in a London hotel.

Bill Young during filming for a US PBS special.

On the set of the *Are You Being Served?* spin-off *Grace and Favour*.

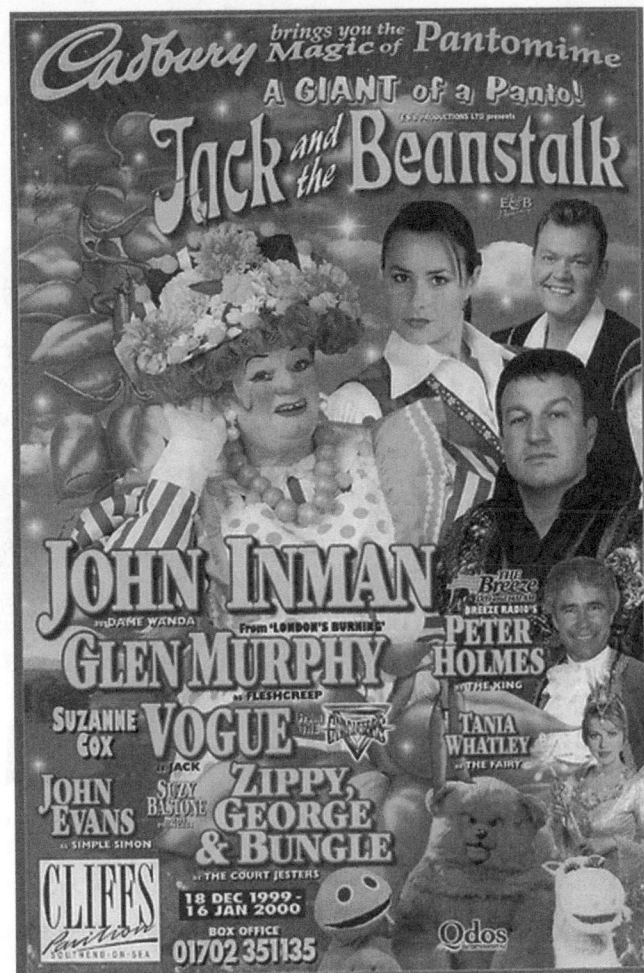

More panto fun in *Jack and the Beanstalk*, towards the end of his panto days …

John and long-time partner Ron Lynch at their civil partnership in December 2005.

Jason Watkins (front centre) and, to his immediate left, Sherrie Hewson in the one-off 2016 BBC remake of *Are You Being Served?* (© BBC)

13

Menswear!

British comedy was continuing to evolve and as the cast of *Are You Being Served?* prepared for a ninth season, so a plethora of new shows were also appearing on TV such as *Blackadder* and *Auf Wiedersehen, Pet*, which were proving hugely popular.

Filming began in March, and it must have been like slipping on a pair of comfortable old slippers for John Inman, who had been involved in numerous plays, pantos and projects since the last series was filmed two years earlier. Six episodes had been commissioned and would be aired between April and May, with John and Mollie continuing as the established stars of the show – a fact confirmed by their salaries, which dwarfed other cast members by comparison.

Doremy Vernon reprised her role as the canteen manageress, but felt the show was, by that stage, in decline:

John was on an astronomical salary, which shows how his popularity grew over the years, and he'd totally overtaken Trevor Bannister, who had almost certainly been earning a lot more than John at the beginning.

I heard Frank Thornton got wind of John's salary and went to see the producers to get his pay more in line, but I was told they informed him that if he didn't like it, he could leave.

I thought *Are You Being Served?* diminished as time went on, especially when they started dressing Mollie and John up in various costumes and outfits. They didn't need props to get their laughs – they were as funny in the read throughs as they were during filming.

At the end of each series, we'd have an end of production party, and it would be held at John's home house in Little Venice, which was much friendlier than having it in a BBC rehearsal room. It was quite extraordinary to be in a modern house in Little Venice, which was almost exclusively old properties, but we had some lovely times there.

Ratings may have been falling, but there was still a sizeable and loyal following who loved the show, even if the scripts and format were becoming somewhat tired.

John had accepted an offer to perform *Pyjama Tops* for a third time from June 1983 onwards, and it would give the opportunity of spending the summer in Jersey, with the show being held at the Opera House on the beautiful Channel Island. When assembling the cast, John thought of Fay Hillier, who had only recently lost her partner Dick Emery, with the comic actor dying of heart failure aged 67. Hillier said:

Dick died in January 1983, and it had been a terrible shock. Not long after, Bill Roberton, John's manager and agent and somebody I'd worked with a few years before, called me up and asked if I wanted to read for part in John's play *Pyjama Tops*.

It was only three months since Dick's death and I told them I couldn't cope, I was crying easily and was not myself at all, but then John spoke to me personally and asked why didn't I just come up and see if something could be done, so I did.

But when I arrived to meet John and Bill, I spoke three lines of the part they were offering and then burst into tears. I could barely breathe let alone read anything. John completely understood and told me to get myself home and was sorry to have caused me any distress. Of course, when I got home I regretted what had happened because I only really worked with Dick and needed a job.

The part went to another actress on this occasion and John would once again play Leonard Jolly, with Andrew Knox cast as George Charles, and the rest of the cast included Janet Edis, Shirley Cheriton and Nicholas Field.

For a period during the run, John had to hand the baton to Melvyn Hayes due to filming commitments. Hayes, one of the stars of the long-running BBC sitcom *It Ain't Half Hot Mum*, recalls his brief stint stepping into John's sizeable shoes:

I took over from John because he was going off to do a TV series and he said that the night before I started, he wanted to introduce me to the audience after the show, which I thought was a very generous gesture.

So, he did the show and then explained it was his last one and then introduced me on stage. The audience applauded and when it died down, I said, 'Ladies and gentlemen, we have a saying in our business that you should never leave the stage cold – meaning when you say your last line, you should never take it into the wings, and you should always turn back to the audience to keep the stage warm.'

I then added, 'All I can say about the way John has been tonight and his behaviour on the stage is, it ain't half hot, mum!' It was very cheesy!

In David Croft's autobiography, he revealed that they were thinking of casting John Inman as the Gloria character I eventually became in *It Ain't Half Hot, Mum*, but he was busy doing something else, then Croft went on to say, 'but Melvyn Hayes was free!' John would have been brilliant in it, but he'd established himself so strongly in *Are You Being Served?*, it might have been difficult for viewers to see him as somebody else.

I recall David and Jeremy were very worried that John was going to go off and do his own thing with a series of summer specials on

TV, but they never took off and David called Jeremy when he discovered it wasn't going to mean they'd lose John and asked if he'd heard the news? Jeremy said yes, have *you* heard the news? David then said, 'Yes, and there's a song in my heart.' John was so integral to *Are You Being Served?* that they were terrified of losing him.

I was so nervous on my first night, I cut the performance time by fifteen minutes – not because I missed out dialogue, just because I said it twice as fast! John told me that he did a spot in the middle of the show when he did it and that I might enjoy doing it as well – it was his own personal business and so I asked what it was. He said, 'Well, halfway through the show I spot a bowl of crisps at the side of the stage and go over and pick it up. I break out of character, tell the audience I'm so hungry because they don't feed me that well, and then go into the audience and start offering crisps while telling funny stories about Jersey.'

I told him that I'd love to do that, and I did – it was the first time I'd tried it, and I really enjoyed it. I got an Irish comedian to supply a few jokes about Jersey, so I wasn't replicating John's act, and it was fantastic. I never did it again, but it was John who came up with that and it was a really nice touch, and it showed his generosity. He was a lovely, funny man.

John returned to complete the season, but it wasn't long before there was the need to replace another member of the cast, though sadly it was a permanent replacement.

Actor Peter Symonds was on tour in another play, but when tragedy struck one of the *Pyjama Tops* cast, he was offered the opportunity of taking on a role that had been vacated in the most awful of circumstances. He recalled:

In August 1983, I finished a three-month national tour of the Alan Bennett play *Habeas Corpus*, which starred Patsy Rowlands and the comedy actor Jack Douglas, brother of John's agent Bill Roberton.

As well as taking care of John's career, Bill also directed many of John's pantos and touring shows and had directed that year's summer season at the Opera House theatre, Jersey, with John starring in *Pyjama Tops*.

John had appeared in the show during its run in London a few years earlier, where it had had a glass swimming pool on stage into which several extraneous, but very pretty girls in skimpy swimwear dove at various points in the action for no apparent reason other than, presumably, to entice in a mainly male audience – the sort of clientele usually found at the Windmill Theatre and various insalubrious Soho strip joints.

The Jersey production dispensed with the pool and the bevy of beautiful young ladies altogether and played the piece as the bedroom farce it was originally intended to be. In Jersey, John, by sheer force of his comic brilliance, extracted every ounce of fun out of it, denuding it of any of its previous salaciousness, and turning it into great family entertainment.

He incorporated lots of asides to the audience, poked good-humoured fun at the other actors, making each of them (and me, in my turn) corpse at several points during the show. Cod corpses subsequently became part of the show each night. Needless to say, the audience loved it. The actors not always quite so much!

Playing the wayward husband George Charles – John's character's best friend and confidante – was the actor Andrew Knox (son of the famous British film actor of the 1950s, Alexander Knox). Clearly, Andrew was in a very unhappy place in his life, and one day went missing. John and the rest of the cast were shaken to the core to learn subsequently that Andrew had committed suicide by throwing himself overboard from the Jersey ferry. A very young assistant stage manager – an unrehearsed and unprepared understudy – had to go on in his place for several performances, but it was clear immediately that a proper professional replacement was called for.

I never quite understood exactly how it was that I came into the frame. Presumably Bill Roberton must have told his brother, Jack Douglas, of the tragedy and the show's resultant problem and Jack must have suggested me to take over. I was contacted on a Friday afternoon, and flew out to Jersey on the Saturday morning, having never seen the show, or even read a script.

I met John for the first time after seeing the show for the first time that evening, went through the blocking [positioning] with the company manager on the Sunday morning followed by lunch at John's rented house where he was, for that week, playing host to Wendy Richard and her then partner. I watched the show again, still with the young assistant stage manager understudy playing George, on the Monday and Tuesday evenings and went on stage for the first time on Wednesday evening, only having had one run through with the entire cast that afternoon, getting through the show with perhaps a little too much caution, but otherwise without incident.

Afterwards, John came to my dressing room. 'Well done,' he said, then added, 'It was a bit slow!'

I took the comments to heart and must have ended up playing what was a hard-working, sweat-inducing, frantic, rush-around feed for John to his satisfaction!

Pyjama Tops was another hit with audiences and at the box office, but when the summer season finished, John and Ron returned to London and prepared for his annual panto appearance as *Mother Goose*, which this year would be held at the Birmingham's Alexandra Theatre and was his thirteenth appearance in a Christmas production.

Meanwhile, a tenth – and final – season of *Are You Being Served?* had been commissioned and filming would begin in May 1984, although in order to fit around various schedules, filming for the six episodes started on 13 May and ended on 27 July, and the series would not be aired until February 1985. The urgency to screen the show certainly wasn't prevalent among the BBC executives.

For production manager Susan Belbin, it was also time to move to pastures new. She said:

I stayed with *Are You Being Served?* for nine years and worked with David Croft on whatever he was doing.

Because Robin Nash, who was the head of comedy at the time, had spoken with David Croft, I was presented with the chance to direct Carla Lane's *Bread* and told to 'get on with it'. After that, I left David and worked on *Only Fools and Horses*, *One Foot in the Grave*, *It Ain't Half Hot Mum*, and later, *Jonathan Creek*.

In years to come, David Liddament offered me the role of executive producer of light entertainment at the BBC ... that meant also keeping an eye on BBC Scotland, BBC Wales, but I wasn't sure, and David looked more than a little surprised when I said I'd need to go away and think about it.

But after three days of hard thinking, I accepted the job – but shortly after, my husband had a back operation that went badly wrong. He needed looking after and so I left the BBC in 1996 and would probably have been the Controller now, but I needed to look after my husband.

Once the last episode had been recorded, John set off for another summer season of *Pyjama Tops*, this time at the Gaiety Theatre for a three-month stint in Douglas, Isle of Man.

A new run in the hugely popular play also gave the opportunity for John to contact Fay Hillier again to see if she was ready to work. It had been more than twelve months since Dick Emery's death, and she recalls a phone call from John in the spring of 1984 – and what would be the start of a close friendship that would last for the next twenty-three years:

John called me himself and asked, 'Are you feeling better? Would you like to come in and read for the play?' I had got myself together and I was feeling better, so I went to see him and ended up working with John for almost six years, mostly in *Pyjama Tops*.

We toured all over England, the Channel Islands, and the Isle of Man. It was so successful. I initially joined when it played in the Isle of Man, and I got to know and love John as time went on.

I'd worked with many comics as a feed and if I got a laugh, they would take that line out because they wanted to get the laughs.

Benny Hill was like that, and Bernie Winters nearly sacked me once for getting a better laugh than he did! John was never like that. If you got a laugh, he'd say, 'Well done, darling – let's keep that in,' and he'd explain, 'Look, my name might bring people in but it's all of us who send them home happy.'

He was more generous than any actor I ever worked with.

It was interesting, because he told me would have loved to have a family and that there was a girl he fell for in his 20s, but he just couldn't make it work for him physically – it had to be a man.

He loved to have women friends, but he had to have women friends who knew where he was at, so to speak. I used to go to the Rats Ball with him regularly because he wanted to have somebody with him, and he couldn't go with Ron.

Ron would have a female partner and John would have me. Some of my girlfriends used to say, 'Have you got him into bed yet, darling?' and I'd joke, 'No, not yet – still trying!'

He loved Ron dearly, but Ron was a bit naughty from time to time! I remember John telling me Ron was upset over something or other, so he had to go out and buy him a diamond to make everything alright again, which he did.

He was the nicest, kindest man and he had the happiest company I've ever worked with in my life – and I've worked with a lot. John just kept everyone amused and if there ever was an issue, he'd just make everyone laugh and we'd get over it immediately and he was just brilliant at smoothing out any problems.

Wherever we were playing, he'd hire a house out for the duration with a garden because he loved doing a barbecue for everyone on a Sunday – showbiz friends, friends, family, and he loved a big get together, wearing a minimal bikini and we always thought he would scorch something badly one day!

There is an awful lot of hierarchy in the theatre and a lot of actors won't talk to stage hands and all that sort of nonsense, but every night after each show, all the stage hands and backstage people came out and we went and had a lovely dinner together each and every night – and I think that's what made the company so happy, because everyone felt equal. John understood the people who were often forgotten and in the background were just as important as the actors on the stage and he made them feel part of the team and important. He was an extraordinarily kind man.

Rejoining the cast in Douglas had been Peter Symonds, who was offered the chance to reprise the role of George Charles that he'd enjoyed so much the year before with John in Jersey. He didn't need to think about the offer too long:

I must have done OK, for John asked me to repeat the role the following summer, 1984, for a three-month season in Douglas. It was while we were playing there that John was asked to play Frank Randle – a famous forties music hall comedian who he had idolised since he was a young man – in an episode of a TV series called *Super Troupers*, which saw modern-day celebrities recreate the acts of great music hall artists of the past. For example, Vivian Pickles played Gracie Fields and Sheila Steafel, Marie Lloyd and so on. In our *Pyjama Tops* cast was a young actor called John Field – son of the famous music hall comic Sid Field. I imagine, it was a suggestion of John Inman's that he and John Field recreate one of his father's best-known sketches and I was roped in to play Sid's long-time friend and feed, actor Jerry Desmond, who, after Sid's death went on to work in the same feed capacity in numerous films with Norman Wisdom.

John, along with Ron Lynch, who always acted as his dresser and personal assistant, John Field, and me, all flew together one Sunday afternoon in a private plane to Newcastle to recreate and record the two acts at an old music hall theatre in front of a live audience.

The show, directed by Royston Mayo, would be screened the following March. Our return to the Isle of Man by the same plane was scheduled for the next day, but, taxiing down the runway, the flight suddenly had to be abandoned when warning lights and sirens flashed indicating a problem with the engine. We were marooned at Newcastle Airport for some hours while repairs were carried out, and only narrowly avoided missing that evening's performance. None of us found the subsequent flight back – through heavy cloud – a relaxing experience!

Time was moving on and that year finished as so many before it had, with panto and yet another production of *Mother Goose*, this time at the Churchill Theatre in Bromley.

As he approached his 50th birthday, John Inman and Wilberforce Clayborne Humphries were about to go their separate ways, at least for now …

14

End of an Era or Start
of a New One?

John Inman's farewell to *Are You Being Served?* began on 18 February 1985 in the episode 'Goodbye Mrs Slocombe' and ended with 'The Pop Star' – the final and sixty-ninth episode of a programme that had first aired thirteen years earlier. It was a remarkable run for a show that had made stars of all its cast, and John into one of the nation's biggest and most bankable names. Although there would be no more recordings, *Are You Being Served?* was a long way from being finished – which would be particularly good news for Mr Humphries.

John would feature regularly on TV throughout the year, appearing in *The Good Old Days* several more times, where he was able to perform many of his vaudeville routines to an appreciative audience. He was also a firm favourite on a number of panel shows, particularly Bob Monkhouse's *Celebrity Squares* on ITV. His performance in *Super Troupers* as Frank Randle aired in March 1986 and he was enjoying the variety of offers his fame had brought him.

Peter Symonds was delighted to get the chance to work with John for a third year in a row for a new play that was set for a lengthy tour. He said:

John and I had become great friends and, as everyone who ever worked with him knows, he was extremely generous and loyal. As a result, in early 1985, he asked me to play in a new comedy called *Bedside Manners* which, again directed by Bill Roberton, opened with a four-week run at Salisbury Playhouse on 16 March and then continued on a long tour, which included another four weeks in Douglas on the Isle of Man, and weeks in Harlow, Wolverhampton, Hull, Southsea, Newark, Eastbourne, Worthing, Hanley, Margate and Dartford.

John knew that, in addition to acting, I also directed, and once the play had opened, he would discuss comic business with me and allow me to make suggestions, which he always took on board without any sense that he was the big star and knew all there was to know about comedy. He was thrilled by any suggestions the other actors inserted into the show and would stand in the wings laughing delightedly, knowing that the effect was to keep the audience warmed up and happy so that they felt they'd had a wonderfully enjoyable evening for which he was responsible.

For me, the most fascinating thing about him as an actor in both shows was that he was totally aware that his Mr Humphries persona was why audiences had come to see him, but once he made his initial appearance in the Mr Humphries vein and satisfied them that he was *that* John Inman, he proceeded very subtly to leave the Humphries character behind and create an entirely different comic one that made them laugh just as much and appreciate his enormous comic versatility.

Sadly, Bill Roberton was a not as ambitious for John as he should have been and allowed – and indeed, encouraged him – to go on hoeing the same furrow when, in fact, I believe he could have proved himself as a great comic actor in some of the classic comic roles such as Moliere's *The Miser* or the many dandies in Restoration Comedy.

The eighteen-week run of *Bedside Manners* had taken up the lion's share of 1985 for John, who celebrated his 50th birthday during the tour. Fay Hillier was on hand to help him celebrate:

On tour, I was the company cake maker and made cakes for everybody's birthday. When we were at Devonshire Park, for the 100th performance, the company theatre people wanted a cake to celebrate.

I also made a 50th birthday cake for John – it was blue with as many candles as I could get around it – not quite 50! – and after the show, we were going to a restaurant to celebrate so I asked if they could store it in a nice, cool place. In their infinite wisdom, they decided to put it in the freezer! It was completely rigid when they brought it to the table and John posed for a picture when he was about to cut it with this terrified look on his face because it was frozen solid.

John would pop up in the Christmas edition of Les Dawson's *Blankety Blank* – in full panto regalia of course – which was shown on BBC1 on 27 December – but at that actual time, he was back in panto at Stockport's Davenport Theatre.

It seemed that he'd had his fill of *Mother Goose* for the time being and instead for this panto season he played Aladdin, who appeared to be a not-too-distant relative of Mr Humphries. He played alongside Roy Barraclough, who took on dame duties as Widow Twankey, and a stellar cast that included Jack Douglas, Nicholas Brent and Janette Beverley. It was directed, as so many of John's stage shows were, by Bill Roberton.

The following year, 1986, would be another productive one. Though it would be dominated by a four-month run of *Pyjama Tops* at the Devonshire Theatre in Eastbourne and finish with a week at the Richmond Theatre, there were other interesting opportunities opening up for John Inman – while another one was about to end for an old friend.

At some stage that year, John received a call from a BBC producer, concerned that his old friend Barry Howard's drinking and belligerence had become intolerable to the cast and crew on *Hi-Di-Hi!* A friend of John's, who wishes to remain anonymous, recalled:

Although I always associate John with Barry Howard because they were a fantastic pantomime duo, it was a great sadness that Barry clearly envied John's huge success. When Barry found his own fame on *Hi-Di-Hi!*, we thought they could stand side by side again, equally admired for their talent. But, sadly, Barry became very grand and unpopular with his cast – and the management. He increased his drinking until he became a liability. The BBC were unable to cope with this and sought John's help and advice, asking what they should do? John immediately said, 'Sack him.' The BBC, I'm sure, were relieved to have this back-up from John, who was the consummate professional.

Howard's time in the spotlight was about to end and John's honest stance on the matter was probably down to his professionalism rather than personal reasons. It's hard to imagine anything else or that he was taking the opportunity to take some sort of payback as, by all accounts, they were no longer in touch and hadn't been for some time.

It was possibly an appearance on veteran Radio 2 DJ Mike Craig's show *It's a Funny Business* that convinced BBC Radio bosses that John was a natural broadcaster. In the interview with Craig, John effortlessly recalled his past with the ease of a natural storyteller, plus his voice was already known to millions. With his connections in showbiz, BBC producer Richard Wilcox was keen to explore the idea of giving him his own show on BBC Radio 2 – and he had an additional ace up his sleeve with friend and former writer of numerous material for John, Tony Hare. Hare recalled in 2023:

> It was in mid-1986 when Richard Wilcox asked me whether he thought I could get John on the radio and I said I didn't know but I could ask his agent.
>
> He said, 'It'd be better if you called him, being a friend', so I agreed and gave him a ring and he was quite interested in the idea but said he didn't know how radio worked.

Initially, John was apprehensive about the possibility of broadcasting, having never done anything of his own on radio before. But when he learned Tony would be penning various sketches and guiding him along, he soon warmed to the idea. Hare continued:

I told him he didn't have to learn the lines because he would just need to read them from the script and after convincing him to take it on, I was commissioned to write the series that we'd call *Inman and Friends*.

It was funny because John called me a few days later and said, 'Tony, the contracts department have just called and the money is dreadful!'

I told John I should have warned him about that, but that it was great fun and only a day's work for each show, and he said he hadn't thought about it like that. I'd been working on the long-running radio show *The Huddlines* with Roy Hudd – something I did for twenty-two years – and we went ahead and did the series and had guests like Kenneth Connor and Ernie Wise and we had a great time. Sherrie Hewson and Jeff Holland were regulars and later Sally Grace stepped in; they were all hysterical.

It was very popular and went out in the afternoon, but later the evenings – it was a bit naughty for a lunchtime slot! We used to go the Captain's Cabin after each show for drinks and it was a joy to know John and work with him again. We had a lot of fun on that series.

He was arguably at the peak of his fame at that time and I went to see him at the Cromwell Hospital in London where he was having his varicose veins done and he asked if I wanted a drink. I said I wouldn't mind and asked should I call the matron to get us both a cup of tea and he said, 'Tea? Tea? I've got a minibar next to my bed!' It was a plush, private clinic, of course, so we sat there having a gin and tonic in his private room. Very John Inman!

Inman and Friends began with an initial eight-week season, running from 30 September to 18 November 1986.

With so many showbusiness friends, John was able to line up a list of stellar guests that included Ernie Wise as the first guest, then best pal Wendy Richard, Bobby Crush, Arthur English, Ruth Madoc, Peggy Mount, George Chisholm and Kenneth Connor. Speaking to the *Radio Times* in 1986, John described the show:

It's definitely not alternative humour. You could call it old-fashioned, even.

Each programme starts with me saying 'Hasn't it been a funny sort of day?' and going on about it. Then I introduce my guests … they really *are* friends. They include the various members of the Grace Brothers gang, and the likes of Ernie Wise, Ruth Madoc, and Peggy Mount. We chat, do gags, sketches, I sing in a strangled tenor …

Recorded in front of a live studio audience, it was, as he described, a mixture of chat and sketches, with John employing the services of Sherrie Hewson and Jeffrey Holland as his co-hosts. Hewson recalls:

We worked together on *Inman and Friends* on Radio 2 for a few years and had the most wonderful time with amazing guests. Jeffrey and I would join John and because it was him, we had people like Ernie Wise come on and a whole host of top names because they all loved him, and he could command that calibre of guest.

Co-host Holland agreed the show was a delight to be involved with:

Working with John on *Inman and Friends* on Radio 2 with Sherrie was a wonderful time, and we had a lot of laughs and met some really eminent celebrity performers as guests on the show.

John was a very funny man on and off stage with a ready sense of humour and a waspish wit about him, which I suppose is why he and Barry Howard had got on so well for so many years! I'd been lucky enough to appear with John in an early episode of *Are You Being Served?* called 'The Apartment'.

Later, when I got the role as Spike in *Hi-De-Hi!* and became friends with Barry Howard, he told me that John actually quite fancied me at the time! Typically, Barry went on to add though that I did absolutely nothing for him!

The recordings were done at the Paris Studio in Lower Regent Street, which is sadly long gone now and has been replaced with a fitness centre! The half-hour shows usually took about an hour to get through. I remember meeting Kenneth Connor for the first time on John's show. It was a treat for me as I had talked the writers into recreating his character Sidney Mincing which he used to do on *Ray's a Laugh* with Ted Ray when I was growing up!

John never did appear with me and Barry on *Hi-de-Hi!* as he was already well established on *Are You Being Served?* by then. I discovered he and Barry were not so close as they had been as Barry was somewhat put out when John's fame meant he was asked to do Dame roles in panto instead of one half of the Ugly Sisters, so Barry had to find a new sister for his act. Of course, when Barry himself achieved renown in *Hi-De-Hi!*, things were mollified somewhat.

Hewson, who had appeared in *Carry On Behind* and dozens of comedy and drama shows over the years, jumped at the chance of being one of John's wing men:

I knew Jeff already and when John invited us to be part of *Inman and Friends*, it was an easy decision. We'd be part of the sketches and also chat with guests who all loved being part of it and they almost always asked if they could come back for more. John was so easy-going and would let Jeff and I do whatever we wanted.

One guest Hewson had been keen to work with left her feeling a little sad, with the appearance of somebody she'd admired for many years turning out to be a little more difficult than the team had anticipated:

Ernie Wise's appearance was a strange one and he was our very first guest. He was still recovering from losing Eric Morecambe and was now on his own, and as the straight man of the pair – to a degree – the transition from being a duo to a single act is very difficult. Eric and Ernie were so huge, and we were thrilled when Ernie agreed to appear.

When he arrived for recording, we sat down with him and went through how we intended to start the show off and the sketches we had planned but Ernie just went, 'No, no … we won't be doing that.'

John, sensing the moment, subtly said to Jeff and me, 'You go off and get ready kids and I'll go through this with Ernie.' We had an idea what he was doing, which was to nail down exactly what Ernie *was* happy doing, and ultimately he did no sketches, just a stand-up spot alone because it was sort of 'I'm Ernie Wise', but it just didn't work without Eric. We wanted to just have a fun time with him and wouldn't have taken anything away from his act, but although I understood his dilemma because of the enormity of his relationship with Eric, it just made the whole thing a bit awkward.

Later in the pub, John said it didn't matter and that it had all been good. He said he understood where Ernie was coming from and had complete empathy with him, as he did with everybody. He wouldn't backbite or have a bad word about anyone, and he completely got Ernie's plight and professional and personal loss.

The Paris Studios had a fantastic history and it used to be a cinema, so you had to go downstairs to get to it. *I'm Sorry I Haven't a Clue* and the radio production of *Dad's Army* were all recorded there. There was a little hatch where you got tea and cakes and there was a big stage – it was a brilliant place to work, and John absolutely loved being there. After recording, we'd always go to a little old pub down the road and it was the best of times, it really was.

Our second guest was Wendy Richard, who he adored and had she still been with us she could have shared endless tales about her and John, mainly based around champagne in a Baker Street pub in London! They were brilliant together and that was a partnership made in heaven.

We live in quite a selfish world these days, but John was probably the most unselfish person I ever met as a friend and as an artist because he'd allow other comics to be funny – and a lot of comics won't do that because they are the funny ones who surround themselves with straight men to feed them the laughs. I was the 'straight man' when I worked with Russ Abbot and it was an accepted role, but John would allow and encourage you to be funny and get the laughs. He'd have others come on stage and get the tag line and the last laugh, and there's not many comics I know who would allow that. John never bothered and it didn't worry him – as long as people were laughing and everyone was having fun, that was enough for him.

John was Mr Humphries and Mr Humphries was John Inman. He was that character and brought himself totally and utterly to Mr Humphries and everything he did, every little affectation, movement and reaction was John. It was brilliant and whenever I'm talking to students, I tell them to watch John Inman and his timing. It wasn't something you can really teach, he had naturally funny bones, but timing is something you either have or you don't, and his timing was perfect. He could time a gag to perfection with or without an audience and was a force to be reckoned with on screen, on stage or on film. If you were in a scene with John, forget it because he would steal it. And not for selfish reasons, he was just that talented.

By the time the first series *of Inman and Friends* had ended, it was time to start preparing for panto again. John once again appeared in *Aladdin*, this time as Dame Widow Twankey, with Irish comic Jimmy Cricket as Wishee Washee and Jessica Martin as Aladdin. The first show was on 23 December at the Grand Theatre, Wolverhampton, and played to sold-out audiences during the season.

What Jimmy and John hadn't realised was that they had worked together before, but not on stage, although there had never really been any mention of it anywhere previously. Cricket, a huge star of the 1970s and '80s and a tireless worker for charitable causes, recalled – like so many before him – that working with John had been an enjoyable experience:

It was *Aladdin* in 1986 at the Grand Theatre in Wolverhampton that we worked together, and I played Wishee Washee to John's Widow Twankey.

He was one of the best dames in the country. He had an amazing array of costumes that got more outrageous as the panto progressed. I remember one outfit in particular that looked like a zebra crossing complete with a Belisha beacon on his head that lit up. It used to floor the audience every time he made his entrance with it on ...

During that panto run John and I did an interview together for a local radio station and to our astonishment we discovered we'd both worked in a large department store in London in the '60s called Gamages. John had been a window dresser and I had worked up in the toy department demonstrating a trick pack of cards. Obviously, his stint in Gamages – which must have been before Austin Reed – had held him in good stead for when he got his TV break.

John was a lovely guy and that was borne out by the fact that on the last night of the panto, for some inexplicable reason, I found myself with no money to buy petrol for the journey back to Rochdale – I didn't use credit cards back then. Unhesitatingly, John lent me the money. On the Monday morning I sent him back the money to his home in London. I still remember his address in Little Venice.

The famous song from South Pacific goes 'There is Nothing Like a Dame!' – well there was no one like John Inman. It was a pleasure to share the stage with him.

It had been another wonderful twelve months for John, but unbeknownst to this most versatile comic actor, an Anglophile TV executive across the Atlantic was going to introduce Mr Humphries, Mrs Slocombe and the rest of the *Are You Being Served?* cast to millions of new fans. America was about to fall in love with John Inman.

15

American Dreams

During the early part of 1987, John Inman left the UK to embark on a lengthy tour of the Middle East and Far East in the play *My Fat Friend*, following that up with a comprehensive tour of New Zealand during the summer, starring in *Pyjama Tops*.

Panto, plus game shows, guest appearances and time with friends and Ron took up the rest of the year. He adored time at home in Little Vencie and enjoyed the company of his many showbusiness friends.

Over in Dallas, a confirmed lover of English comedy was on the hunt for new shows to export to the States, and that's when he came across *Are You Being Served?* Bill Young is today the head of programming for a PBS station in Dallas called KERA. The moment he watched *Are You Being Served?*, he was hooked. He could feel in his gut that US viewers would love this quintessentially British sitcom and so he set about negotiating with the BBC. He explained:

PBS is the sort of equivalent of the BBC in the US, with each state having its own public broadcasting system, with the main difference being that each individual city has its own PBS station.

Our schedule will be somewhat different from New York, which is somewhat different from Los Angeles, which is somewhat different to Chicago and so on. They are largely the same pro-grammes, and we buy a lot of BBC programmes as well as ITV shows and, as time went on, Channel 4 and Channel 5, to sup-plement the PBS schedule, which are the nationally distributed programmes. My role, specifically, is to acquire the programmes, buy and schedule them for Dallas and north Texas. Yes, I get paid to watch TV every day!

We were the first US TV station to broadcast *Monty Python* in 1974 and I often say you can either thank us or yell at us for bring-ing British comedy over, though I'm certain it would have come over sooner or later.

We bought *Are You Being Served?* for the first time in 1987 and it quickly became popular with our viewers. The set-up of the show was something that you could translate into all the department stores across the US and *Are You Being Served?* is, I'd have to say, in my top five of UK comedies with *Fawlty Towers* top along with *The Two Ronnies*, *Yes Minister* and maybe *The Fall and Rise of Reginald Perrin*.

The show had already been incredibly popular in Australia and the Netherlands, but the US was a whole different animal, and it would steadily build a cult following throughout 1987 and beyond.

Former show production manager Susan Belbin admits that being big in America was not something she ever envisaged happening for *Are You Being Served?* She said, 'I was marginally surprised it became so successful over there because I wouldn't have thought a gay man waltzing around the TV screen would be an American thing, if that makes sense. But good on them for embracing it.'

For the first time in many years, the panto John selected for 1987 would not see his name adorning the top of the bill posters. For the lavish production of *Babes in the Wood* at the London Palladium, no less, John would take third billing on the pre-production post-ers, with Cannon and Ball headlining and Marti Webb second. John shared equal billing with close pal Barbara Windsor and Derek Griffiths for the eleven-week run that would start just before Christmas and finish at the end of February 1988. He would play the role of Nurse Wanda in a show that would be watched by almost 100,000 people during its lengthy run.

Susan Belbin went to one of the shows at the Palladium but without letting him know she'd be in the audience. However, John soon knew she was there – and made sure she knew he knew! She said:

> One of the last times I saw John was when he was playing on stage in *Babes in the Wood*, and I was laughing my head off because he was so funny and he suddenly stopped midstream and said, 'I can hear you Suzie Belbin!' That was typical John.

During John's days off from panto, he would record a second series of *Inman and Friends* on Radio 2, once again with Sherrie Hewson and Jeff Holland. The eight-week season aired between 7 January and 25 February 1988.

His guests this time were very much *Carry On* influenced as Bernard Bresslaw, June Whitfield, Barbara Windsor and Kenneth Connor all appeared, as well Pat Coombs, Su Pollard and Windsor Davies. Best pal Wendy Richard also featured for the second time.

It proved a popular Thursday evening show with listeners, who were delighted to learn a third series would be aired in December later that year.

Su Pollard was at the height of her *Hi-De-Hi!* fame when she appeared on the show and had become a close friend to John and Ron, enjoying various events and lunches during the twenty years they were friends. They had met not long before and got along like a house on fire. She recalled:

> I first met John when I was still working on *Hi-De-Hi!*. He had finished *Are You Being Served?* by that time and we were at a charity function of some kind, and we just hit it off. John suggested that we should maybe meet up again soon and go and get a cup of tea somewhere soon, and we did – that's how our friendship started.
>
> We did a Royal Variety Performance together – or something similar – and also worked together a number of times on *The Good*

Old Days, which he loved doing. John was proper old school in that he started in the am drams and variety shows, so that was his background, and he was so good in panto and such a genius creating his own props.

I remember one time he had a galleon on his head, and he had this mechanism that made it wobble about in the storm. He was so inventive.

He also had the infamous 'fun room' at the top of his house in Little Venice, and he was very generous in his hospitality, and he'd say, 'Come on over I'm having another do at the fun room!' There was a bar in there, music and he was such a generous host.

I think he learned a lot off Danny La Rue – and I did a bit – because whenever we'd go backstage to see Danny after a show, he'd always go 'Come in, come in, my darlings, come into my dressing room and take a seat,' and he'd have a bottle of Lanson champagne in a bucket of ice. He told us that it was important to give people the whole experience because they would have seen the show and if they got to come into the 'inner sanctum' it should be memorable because they would never usually get to see things like that. John learned from that and always tried to pass that on and make people's experiences lovely.

I went to see him in summer season on Bournemouth Pier and afterwards we'd go to Sandbanks Hotel. John would always take the lead when we were deciding what to do and say, 'Oh no, we're not going there – we need to go somewhere posh!' I don't think he ever stepped in a Wetherspoons! I'd occasionally wind him up by phoning him out of the blue and say, 'John, I've booked us a table for lunch,' and he go, 'Oh darling, where?' I'd tell him it was a Wetherspoons on the High Street, and he'd say, 'Oh, I've just looked at my diary and I can't make it!' He was so funny, a good bloke and really nice friend to have.

John accepted the offer of a brief cameo in Richard Curtis' movie *The Tall Guy*, starring Rowan Atkinson, Jeff Goldblum and Emma Thompson – a first appearance on the silver screen since the *Are*

You Being Served? movie, and the £3 million budget for the film was almost doubled at the box office. He was open to anything and everything if it piqued his interest, but he also enjoyed working with people he genuinely had time for.

As a case in point, rising talent Gary Wilmot had launched his own entertainment show *Cue Gary!* in 1988 on ITV. A former contestant on the talent show *New Faces*, Wilmot was making his way in the industry and when he was discussing a sketch in his show that required the character of a flustered film director, he recalled a meeting with John Inman a few years earlier and the producers suggested John Inman might be ideal. Recalls Wilmot:

> I'd first met John when he was at the Apollo Theatre in Oxford in panto.
>
> My girlfriend at the time was one of the dancers in the show and I'd just got my foot on the first rung of the showbiz ladder and was just beginning to get noticed, so I arranged to come and see her in the show, and she asked whether I wanted to meet John Inman afterwards.
>
> I told her 'Yeah, I'd love to' because he was just a brilliant entertainer, so afterwards, she took me backstage and she knocked on his dressing room door. John indicated we should go in and there he was, just sitting there smiling, and he said warmly, 'Hello Gary!' and I just said, 'Hello Mr Inman, it's so nice to meet you.'
>
> He said, 'Would you like a drink?' – as was his wont – but I said I didn't because I was a bit shy and didn't want to outstay my welcome. We had a little chat, and I went on my merry way.
>
> So, a few years later, I got my own TV series, and we had a lot of guests such as Windsor Davies and Graham Stark from *The Pink Panther* movies came on. We needed a very camp film director teacher to play a role in a sketch and teach a class of wannabe directors.
>
> During planning, somebody said, 'Have you thought of John Inman?' I said, 'Oh yes! I met him once and he was lovely – he'd be ideal.'

But as it was a one-day job, I thought he probably wouldn't be interested. However, the booking agents contacted his agent anyway, and I'm delighted to say he said yes.

He came along, and he had quite a complicated piece of dialogue to read out about 'the camera's rolling, has the poodle been to make-up? and lights, camera, action' – that kind of stuff – and he was terrific. After rehearsals, I was sat with him in the canteen, and I told him I was so delighted he was doing this for us because he was ideal for it.

Then he said, 'Do you know why I'm doing it?'

I thought about it and said, 'No, not really – why are you doing it?'

He said, 'Because, Gary, you called me Mr Inman.'

I was chuffed about that, and I get emotional even now thinking about it because it's amazing that such a little bit of respect could be paid back many years later.

I was lucky enough to go on and do panto a couple of times with John after that and I've never seen anyone hold a panto audience in the palm of their hand like John did.

A mix-up in scheduling meant that Sherrie Hewson and Jeff Holland weren't available for the third and final series of *Inman and Friends*, so Sally Grace and Jon Glover stepped in as John's co-hosts.

Although the original team had worked well, Glover and Grace slipped in seamlessly at relatively short notice. In my interview with Sally, she recalled:

I'm not sure quite what went wrong but there was a kerfuffle and producer Richard Wilcox had got all the dates mixed up and he suddenly had to get the third series of *Inman and Friends* out really quickly.

Another producer called Andy Ayliss asked if I could step in as neither Sherrie or Jeff were available.

It was great fun, mainly just sketches and chat, and it went out at the back end of December 1988. The audiences loved it, and we had full houses every time – it held about 220 at the Paris Studios. We turned it around in no time and I found John great company, lovely and very friendly, and I really enjoyed working with him, albeit briefly.

Season 3 of *Inman and Friends* was aired on Radio 2 and began on 8 December 1988, running for eight weeks and had Kenneth Connor, Liz Frazer, Wendy Richard, ventriloquist Ray Allen and Lord Charles, Percy Edwards, Pat Coombs, Graham Stark and Su Pollard.

The year would end, as it almost always did, with a season in panto, this time in *Goldilocks and the Three Bears* at the Grand Theatre in Swansea along with Bruce Montague and David Copperfield. The appeal and workload of John Inman seemed as intense as it had been for getting on two decades, with plenty more to come at home and overseas.

16

'Have You Met My Daughter?'

Derek Benfield's *Bedside Manners* was John Inman's main focus for 1989, starting at the Salisbury Playhouse on 16 March and visiting Douglas for a month before spending weeks in Harlow, Wolverhampton, Hull, Southsea, Newark, Eastbourne, Worthing, Hanley, Margate and finishing on 9 September in Dartford. It involved six long months on the road, playing to strong reviews and sold-out houses wherever it went and featuring Robin Askwith, star of the *Confessions of …* movies, and Louise English.

John and Ron then had a winter break. Often, actress friend and neighbour Noelle Finch would join them if they went for a few weeks in Portugal or wherever for a warm-weather holiday. Christine Ozanne recalls the dedication that Noelle showed towards John, and how close she had become to him:

> She was John's right-hand woman and she served him for many years. She was rather a sad person in many ways because she'd had a torrid, long affair with another woman who had suddenly dropped her. It was such a shock to Noelle that she developed anorexia nervosa and was hospitalised after losing a great deal of weight.
>
> Noelle loved the social life that John led and through that she revived and got much better. She drank heavily, but she was always

available and on his doorstep whenever he called because she had this little sports car and John didn't drive – nor Ron – or even own his own car.

John returned to London feeling refreshed and ready to go, and he was soon back in front of an audience in *Aladdin* at the Churchill Theatre in Bromley for the panto season, where he was once more playing Widow Twankey.

Recorded some months before, he also appeared in Les Dennis' *Christmas Family Fortunes* as part of a star-studded 'family' – all in full panto regalia – that included Jim Bowen, Windsor Davies and Christopher Biggins. Les Dennis:

> John was a delight on *Family Fortunes*. In the afternoon rehearsals he got through to the big money stage. When he came out of the soundproof booth he was wearing a new, lavish dame costume. He got the biggest laugh when he said, 'I've spent the money.' Sadly he didn't get through on the night, so the wonderful gag wasn't transmitted. I loved John. Whenever he introduced me to anyone he'd say, 'Have you met my eldest son?' I miss him.

Bedside Manners had been another successful string to John's bow, but *Pyjama Tops* had served him even better for many, many years and it would especially do so again in 1990. The play began a lengthy tour in Hanley's Theatre Royal on 2 May for a week before moving on to an eleven-week run at the Pier Theatre in Bournemouth, followed by a week each at Manchester's Palace Theatre, Peterborough's Key Theatre and finally Newcastle's Theatre Royal. The run ended on 20 October after more than six months – again.

It was while in Bournemouth that he became friends with Melanie Stace, who had been a co-host on Jim Davidson's *The Generation Game* a few years' earlier. She remembers the start of what would be a lifelong friendship with great clarity:

My story with John started with the 1990 pantomime season, so I would have met him first for auditioning around 1989 for theatre producer Mark Furness, who had two summer season shows that ran from May to October in Blackpool and Bournemouth. Blackpool was doing *'Allo, 'Allo!* and Bournemouth was doing *Pyjama Tops*.

So I went along with my agent Vincent Shaw because he thought I'd be good for the Vicki Michelle role in *'Allo, 'Allo!* I didn't have my equity card at the time and Mark said he was sorry, but without my card, he couldn't give me the part – but added he might still have something for me. So he invited me to his office in Covent Garden a little while later to meet John Inman and I remember him very clearly and suddenly explaining the meeting wasn't about *'Allo, 'Allo!* in Blackpool, it was about *Pyjama Tops* in Bournemouth.

I'm a Hastings girl, so to play Bournemouth was a great opportunity for me, and John's first words to me were, 'She'll do!' John actually wrote my lines for *Pyjama Tops* – because my part of Bridgie didn't exist up to that point, but John wanted me involved so wrote me in so to speak.

He was wonderful and very pivotal and important in my early career. I was 22 and John took me under his wing, and it was a very paternal relationship. He'd often introduce me by saying, 'Have you met my daughter?' in a beautiful way.

So we performed *Pyjama Tops* from May to October with the part he'd written for me, and I was also acting as assistant stage manager and an understudy for three different leads as well as literally making the tea for everyone, which I loved and John also loved, because he loved a nice cup of tea.

After *Pyjama Tops*, John was preparing to go off and ready himself for the panto season because, of course, he was the king of the pantos. I'd always dreamed of playing in panto and being the Principal Boy, because I'm very tall. John asked, 'What are you doing for Christmas, then?', so I said I was off to Scunthorpe to play in *Mother Goose*, and he said that was great. He told me he already had his Principal Boy – Susan Maughan, who sang

'Bobby's Girl' – but added he'd love to see me play Principal Boy at some stage.

After that, *Pyjama Tops* had been so successful that we went on tour and went to Newcastle, Manchester and Peterborough, playing to sold out houses each time. Ron was always there – assisting, supporting or whatever – he was such a warm, lovely person with a welcoming smile, and he was like a favourite uncle to me in many ways. He was a good, supportive friend who was very funny, but a very gentle, quiet, and loving person.

John had a great outlook on life and was just genuinely funny. He told me he was working as a window dresser at Austin Reed's on Oxford Street in London. He says that was where David Croft saw him – whether that was genuine or not I don't know – but during my days as a jobbing actor, I also worked in Harvey Nichols to keep food on the table and each day I'd wake up and tell myself, 'They saw John Inman working as a window dresser at Austin Reed's, so you'll be alright!'

He had some many funny stories about working around the country and one was that he'd been living in digs up north one time with an alcoholic landlord who had dozens of empty beer bottles in the backyard. He told me he was so cold one night that he went out into the yard, collected about thirty empty beer bottles, and filled them one by one with hot water, then surrounded himself with them and a blanket just to keep warm. He glorified in those stories because that's where he came from and that was him paying his dues – but he was telling us because he knew that no matter how successful he'd become, he wanted us to know that he knew what it was like to struggle and make your way in the industry.

My grandmother loved John – he had this power to appeal to people from all walks of life, all ages, and all backgrounds, which at that time wasn't that common. She loved him on *Are You Being Served?* and all the cast members because they were safe and you trusted them.

My dad would come along to the pantos, and he loved John as well. On one occasion, after the show he came with me, John,

Ron and several cast members and we were at the back of a bar on Bournemouth Pier, and it was freezing cold. The bartender came over and said it was almost time to lock up and he was going to lock the toilets, so if anyone wanted to go, now was the time. John just looked up and said thank you – he was always very polite and a gentleman and never did the star turn. But I could see a glint in his eye and then he said, 'Well you don't know if you need to go, do you? By the time we've finished these drinks, well … you don't, do you?' And that was John. My dad has never forgot that mischievous sense of humour. He was a very caring man, and he always kept his eye on me, and I used to wonder, Why me? – why was I so lucky?

After the run, John told me he was going to be performing *Mother Goose* at the Theatre Royal in Brighton and that he wanted me to play Principal Boy. He'd spoken so highly of me, I didn't even have to audition – I just had to go to the Theatre Royal and meet David Land, who was the theatre owner, and he looked at me and said, 'What are you here for?' I said John had asked me to come and present myself and he said, 'OK, you'll do!'

So, thanks to John, I'd got my equity card, had got my first panto under my belt, had half a year in *Pyjama Tops* and now had a major panto to look forward to with him as well.

He told me he really wanted me with him in *Mother Goose* and it was a dream for me to be part of this wonderful cast that included Donald Hewlett, who played Baron Hardup – another wonderful guy – and John was arguably the best Mother Goose I ever saw. We had a lovely time, and it was a great success.

All the cast came to see him perform – Mollie, Wendy, Trevor Bannister – all of them, who all became a second sort of family. They all just loved him. One evening he looked at my Principal Boy and Joanne Sale who I went on with and he said, 'Just look at you. I want gather you up and put you on my mantlepiece!'

We did twelve weeks and it started off my career in earnest because I was never out of work after that, and it was just back-to-back really good jobs, and they got better and better and better.

All the while John was away from *Are You Being Served?*, it seemed as if he was actually becoming more and more famous, with audiences in the US lapping up his antics as Mr Humphries. The show was now being screened all over the country and gaining a sizeable following. He'd get mailbags of fan mail – as did other cast members, though not as many – from the States, and the demand was such that he decided to accept the PBS offer to embark on promotional mini tours of America, where fans would turn out in their hundreds to see the real-life Mr Humphries.

Social activist, editor and author of gay fiction Jack Fritscher hosted an event in San Francisco where, during a walk in the city centre, a cyclist spotted John, who was considered a gay cultural icon on the west coast, and nearly crashed as he shouted, 'I love you Mr Humphries!' Fritscher recalls:

John Inman came to San Francisco and hosted a high tea at the Fairmount Hotel, where he gave a very witty little talk and then engaged all of us in a Q&A.

One politicised person tried to force John to say outright that his Mr Humphries character was gay. John would only say, 'Mr Humphries was raised by women.'

Getting him off the hook of that insistent activist, I asked John one question, which made him sparkle with the joke. I said, 'Mr Inman, Would you please answer the phone?' He shifted his face and body and lifted a pretend phone and announced, deeply: 'Menswear.' He brought down the house. What a fine guy he was, and what a good actor.

Bill Young of KERA PBS in Dallas arranged several of John's visits to Texas, adding:

John was very popular in the States. He'd come over for several days and do events for the station and a lot of larger stations would also have a retail store at one of the malls that sold a lot of PBS merchandise, and we'd take him there to sign autographs and merchandise and the lines to meet him would be five hours long. He was extraordinarily popular, and he'd play his character up really well. He truly loved it and loved meeting generations of fans and to hear their stories of how they'd discovered *Are You Being Served?* and now their kids loved it. And he was just amazed by the numbers turning up to meet him.

Ron was always with John, but he was always in the background. He was very protective and because John would do anything for anybody, he'd sometimes step in and say, 'OK, time to go now.' Ron and I rarely talked, but it was a magical time. The writing across the board in that show was superb.

John came to Dallas maybe four or five times over the years. We'd put him in a hotel near to where we were holding all the events and my main regret of all his visits was one time when I was in an elevator with him going up to an event at the main reception and as we were going up to the top floor he sang the entire theme to *Are You Being Served?* I just wish cell phones existed because it would have been a viral sensation on social media or YouTube.

He was naturally funny. We tried to get him or any of the cast to talk about show bloopers, which are very popular here in the States, but I remember Frank Thornton saying they had a job to do. Whereas US actors liked to play pranks and looked to occasionally mess things up, many Brits came from the stage and theatre and had formal training. They had set times to get things done, it was a job and they wanted to get it right and in the can.

On one tour, John gave a lengthy interview to US talk show host Paul Lyle in Long Island and explained how Mr Humphries had come into being. John explained:

When Mr Humphries first came on the screen, I became a star overnight – after twenty years. And it was true. I'd been working very hard for twenty years and enjoying every minute of it. I was able to go to Woolworths and nobody would say anything to me, but then it was a case of 'Hi John, how are you?'

The fame came in three stages. At first it was, 'That's him from the shop', then 'That's Mr Humphries' and then, 'Ah look, it's John Inman', which is nice when they know your name.

The scripts were finely tuned – David and Jeremy had done a fine job, and it was all very neat. They used to impersonate us as they wrote the scripts, though we never used to see that. Occasionally we'd add something in rehearsals, and they'd include it or say, 'No that's too filthy.'

There was one scene when I was with Mr Lucas and this customer wanted a pullover and he got it stuck over his head, so Mr Lucas had his head bent over and I was stood behind trying to help and Mr Lucas said, 'It's like pulling a Christmas cracker,' and I said, 'Yes it is – I wonder who'll get the novelty?'

I thought there was no way it would get left in, but it was and I couldn't believe it. We laughed a lot and we were like naughty children, and David Croft would get very angry and say, 'Come on, are we doing this or not? Pull yourselves together.'

At the end of the interview, an audience of around 400, who had been totally engaged and enchanted by every word John had said, spontaneously gave him a standing ovation. The respect and adoration was clear to see in a gathering that included people of all ages.

John Inman had achieved fame in the USA without ever actually performing there in any capacity – a rare feat and one he completely relished.

17

The Return of Claybourne Wilberforce Humphries

When the final episode of *Are You Being Served?* had been filmed some years earlier, there was a wrap party for the cast and crew, during which writer David Croft promised the gathered ensemble that, while the series was over, he saw different opportunities for the characters that he intended to resurrect at a future date.

Commitments to *Hi-De-Hi!*, *'Allo, 'Allo!* and the *Hi-De-Hi!* spin-off *You Rang, M'Lord?* meant there was little or no time to create a new show for the staff of Grace Brothers, but once those sitcoms had come to an end, Croft and Jeremy Lloyd set about working on another – and one they'd enthused over for several years – the follow-up to *Are You Being Served?* Of the original cast, Arthur Brough and Harold Bennett had sadly passed away and Trevor Bannister had moved on, leaving Croft and Lloyd a core of John Inman, Wendy Richard, Mollie Sugden and Frank Thornton.

It had been almost twenty years since the *Are You Being Served?* pilot had first been shown and the cast had obviously aged, so when the new concept was formed – it would be called *Grace and Favour* – the writers came up with the premise that the remaining employees of the now closed Grace Bothers would collectively 'inherit' a country manor house that had been purchased by Young Mr Grace, who had borrowed heavily against their pensions. After initially meeting up at the property, they unanimously decide to relocate to the country permanently to try to make the best of the situation with the intention of turning the house into a hotel – as they were otherwise without income in their later years.

John Inman was taking life a little easier by this point – not excessively so – but he was now in his mid-50s, and many of the cast were even older. Mollie Sugden was almost 70 but had worked continuously since (and during) *Are You Being Served?* ended, including five series' of *That's My Boy* on ITV as well as other more short-lived sitcoms. Frank Thornton was 70 and hadn't worked much on TV during the interim, nor had Nicholas Smith. However, perhaps the junior member of the original cast was now arguably one of the biggest stars of the day, with Wendy Richard's career blossoming after her role as Miss Brahms ended. She was now regularly being watched by 20 million viewers in the hit BBC soap *EastEnders*, where she played the dour, straight-talking Pauline Fowler. Wendy had to request permission to be temporarily written out of the show while she filmed the new *Are You Being Served?* spin-off. Filming would begin during the summer of 1991 on location in Tetbury, Gloucestershire.

Mike Berry, who had played Mr Lucas' replacement Mr Spooner for the last three series, was not invited to reprise his character. He recalled:

I wasn't offered a part in *Grace and Favour* – it wasn't that successful, but I would have done it if I'd been asked because I wasn't doing much else at that time and wouldn't have turned it down.

Arthur English was a lovely guy and an old-time comic who ended up in an old folks' home, so he was in no position to return, but John just kept going, Wendy had gone on to *EastEnders* and I went on to panto and live work, but my career slowed down a bit because you do get a bit typecast in an established show like *Are You Being Served?* I hadn't really socialised much outside of filming because we all had our own private lives, and I don't think any of us had the same interests.

Along with Billy Burden and Fleur Bennett, who would play father and daughter resident farmers Morris and Mavis Moulterd, was Joanne Heywood, who had some previous stage work under her belt as well as a handful of television appearances. She was cast as Jessica Lovelock, who was the upper-class former personal secretary of Young Mr Grace and was also one of the inheritors of the manor – thanks to a deathbed promise from her former employer – as well as having financial authority over the others. She remembered:

I successfully auditioned for the role, and I was cast as Miss Lovelock, which was wonderful.

It was a long time ago now, but I seem to remember that, as well as Mike Stephens – the director, who I'd worked with on two series of *First of the Summer Wine* – David Croft and Jeremy Lloyd were also present at the audition. As I knew that the character of Miss Lovelock rode horses, I decided to wear jodhpurs at the audition.

I'd never actually ridden horses! I trained as a dancer, so you tend not to do both. Everyone seemed delighted and Jeremy said 'Ah, so you ride?'... initially, I laughed, neither confirming nor denying, but, in the end I was honest and told them that I didn't ride, but I'd arranged to have some lessons.

As Miss Lovelock also rode a motorbike, I said I wasn't too sure about how to arrange lessons for that! Fortunately they reassured me they would be engaging the services of a stunt double. That turned out to be the late Roy Alon. I'd first met Roy on the children's television series *The Book Tower* when I was about 14 and he'd also worked with him on *First of the Summer Wine*, so our paths had crossed a few times in the intervening years.

Walking into the rehearsal room on the first day *was* daunting but there was such a wonderful atmosphere. For the original cast, it was a reunion of friends, and Fleur, Billy and I were made very welcome.

My first meeting with John was in the rehearsal room on day one. He was *exactly* as I had imagined him to be – warm, friendly, and utterly charming. I don't know that the cast had a leader as such. Of course, there were friendships within the group, and I know he was very close with Wendy Richard. She was definitely happiest when John was around.

John was a born entertainer, so if he was in a scene it was bound to be fun. Fleur's character Mavis had much more screen time with John. As Miss Lovelock, I had more scenes with Frank Thornton's Captain Peacock, but I thoroughly enjoyed the brief moments I did have with John. In one episode, we danced a *pas de deux* as Romeo and Juliet. It was recorded with a studio audience, and they absolutely loved him.

We had more opportunity to socialise when we were on location, as we were all staying in the same hotel, and we would have meals out together. I don't remember Ron being with us on location, but he was in the studio every week for the recordings and always very attentive to John.

While John was back on dame duties in panto at Brighton in *Mother Goose*, *Grace and Favour* was aired for the first time in the UK on 10 January 1992, to mixed reviews. Brian Slade, writing for the website Television Heaven, said:

Grace and Favour was a surprisingly brave move both for its writers and for the BBC. Moving such a large ensemble of characters into a completely new situation was largely untried, particularly with such a length of time between original and follow-up series.

The writers attempted to keep the warmth of the characters but add a little more to their relationships. In an effort to do so, they tried to make the programme more episodic, with running storylines throughout the two series – something they had never done with *Are You Being Served?* In terms of viewing figures, *Grace and Favour* performed well enough.

In an interview on PBS in Long Island, John Inman reflected on the whole experience:

> It was different, and it had to be – we were all older and it showed, no matter how many make-up ladies we had! We were older, so they had to make it older – and calmer – and it was Jeremy Lloyd who put it all together.
>
> I loved it, and I loved Mavis Moulterd. My character had changed and mellowed. For all those years, I minced around the counter with a tape measure around my neck and with the lapse of time I have changed so the character changed, too.
>
> It wasn't difficult to go back to it because it was something new. I knew who Mr Humphries was, or what he had been, so I could carry on with it, but he was a different character. It was very successful at home; I'm not sure what it was like here in the USA.

Grace and Favour was an easy watch and, for the legions of fans of *Are You Being Served?*, it was a chance to see their favourite characters away from the set of Grace Brothers and follow a new set of adventures.

Filming on location was a novelty for the cast, with the interior shots filmed at the BBC in front of a live studio audience. The comedy was gentler and not as manic, but the hierarchal structure that had been so wonderfully observed and mined throughout the ten seasons of *Are You Being Served?* was gone, much to the script's detriment.

Mr Humphries was given plenty of screen time, but less opportunity to use his waspish wit and double entendres, and his relationship with Mavis – half his age – was at odds with everything we knew about Clayton Wilberforce Humphries. Perhaps it was a gentle dig at those John Inman critics who had labelled his character as a stereotypical gay throughout his time at Grace Brothers.

There were plenty of predictable 'Has anyone seen my pussy?' jokes from Mrs Slocombe, Captain Peacock was as letchy as ever, Mr Rumbold was as dithering as he'd ever been and Miss Brahms was, well, Miss Brahms with not much character development.

The first season had done enough to earn another crack and a second series was commissioned. Filming again took place at Tetbury in the summer of 1992 and was aired in the first six weeks of 1993.

But there was bad news on the horizon, and as Jeremy Lloyd told John Inman of his plans for his character, the BBC pulled the plug. *Grace and Favour's* brief twelve-episode run was over, and the cast were none too happy. John recalled in an interview for US TV in 1993:

The BBC axed it in their wisdom, and it was case of 'No, we're not doing anymore.' I was a bit distressed in a way because it left so many things up in the air.

I had a long conversation with Jeremy Lloyd, and he was telling me about the wonderful plans for a third series – this was obviously before he heard the bad news – and that a wedding was all arranged for Mavis and me, and Mrs Humphries was going to visit, which meant I would have to work very hard because I would be playing both roles.

Then Mavis would run off with a boy from the village, leaving Mr Humphries heartbroken. He would then fall into the arms of Mrs Slocombe, with her thinking, 'Now I can get my claws into him.' There was so much good stuff planned – that's why I was upset! Both *Are You Being Served?* and *Grace and Favour* were a very big part of our lives.

Joanne Heywood added, 'I think the fact that a further series wasn't commissioned hit the original cast members even harder than us newer characters. Without another series to look forward to, there wasn't the excitement of getting together again and we gradually lost touch.'

The show was sold to the USA under the name *Are You Being Served Again?* and TV executive Bill Young for KERA in Dallas says that, while it was warmly received, it didn't carry the impact of the original series:

We didn't get the same response from *Are You Being Served Again?* as we did the original because the quality was lacking a little, but it was nice to see the majority of the cast together again.

As for the success of *Are You Being Served?* and the British sitcoms, it was something that was translatable to folks over here. Every state had department stores, everyone has an aunt like Hyacinth Bucket in *Keeping Up Appearances* and *Fawlty Towers* is just fantastic sitcom. We've all had bad experiences at a hotel, so everything was somewhat translated to a point where people could relate to it. The only one that was perhaps more difficult than the rest was *Only Fools and Horses*, which had some great actors that we know very well in the States, but their jobs didn't translate that well over here and the accents were thicker.

As I say, John came over with Mollie a number of times, plus Nicholas Smith on occasion and Trevor Bannister, too, because it remained so incredibly popular in America – and still is. We see a pronounced spike in audience numbers when older shows are shown like *Are You Being Served?*, *Yes Minister* and *Reginald Perrin* over the shows of today. When you look at the BBC output of today, it's more light drama like *Father Brown*, *Death in Paradise* or *Doc Martin*, which is a little comedy within a drama, whereas we've remained with the lighter comedies of yesteryear. I always joked with my contacts at the BBC, 'How exactly did you get ten seasons out of *Two Pints of Lager and a Packet of Crisps?*'

Are You Being Served? is on every week on most of the stations in the US and it has been for years. We're just playing the same episodes over and over again, so everybody at Grace Brothers is our friend. It's like *I Love Lucy* – you know exactly what is going to happen and yet you still laugh. Saturday and Sunday night is British comedy, and you know exactly where and when to tune in.

Although *Grace and Favour* had been cancelled, John Inman was by now 58 and while he had no intention of retiring, he also took a conscious decision to reduce his workload significantly.

During Long Island TV chat-show host Paul Lyle's lengthy inter-view with John, he asked, 'Is John Inman enjoying life?'

He replied:

Yes, he has enjoyed his life and there's not a lot left I still want to do, apart from doing what I'm doing now: getting a few laughs here and there. That's like a drug for me.

I've realised a lot of my dreams and I'm having a ball tripping around the States, and I'll go home and enjoy it all again by telling people about it.

I don't really have any ambitions apart from being a baddie in a Bond movie! I'd like to sit stroking a cat – you notice I said cat! I just want to jog along saying, 'Oh, that's nice – I'll do that,' and suchlike.

If he was entering a sort of semi-retirement, you'd never have guessed it with the immediate years ahead being anything but relaxing …

18

King Rat

With more time on his hands, John accepted the year-long position of King Rat for the Grand Order of Water Rats – an organisation he'd been associated with for a number of years. Much of 1993 would be taken up with various charitable fundraisers, engagements and meetings, with the Order generally quite guarded about how they work. Melvyn Hayes explained:

> I was King Rat later on, but John was King Rat in 1993. It's a stage charity that was formed in 1889 and a bit different from many of the others and you become very involved. It's what we call a 'Cinderella charity' for actors who need help and maybe can't pay their rent or mortgage for a particular month and there were a lot of big names associated with the Water Rats.
>
> We had lodge meetings at a Water Rats-affiliated pub in London on Sunday evenings and there are always new Rats coming in, but in all honesty I don't know many of the names these days. In my time, there were people like Tommy Cooper, Will Hay, Rick Wakeman and Tommy Trinder.

John spoke little of his time as King Rat, and there are rumoured to be bizarre initiation ceremonies that emulate Masonic lodges connected with the Order, but members are sworn to secrecy, leaving nothing more than hearsay and conjecture. What is known is that John undertook the task studiously, helping raise many thousands of pounds in the process.

However, John and Ron's years of heavy smoking were starting to catch up with them, particularly in John's case. He'd suffered from asthma and bronchitis for many years, with the smoking accelerating his breathing issues. So much so, he collapsed at his home in Little Venice that year and was taken to hospital by ambulance.

He was told to quit or cut down his smoking dramatically, and following doctor's orders, a period of convalescence followed. He was forced to give the panto season a miss for Christmas 1993 on medical advice.

For John, 1994 was largely restful with the odd public appearance here and there before he continued his annual stint in panto, this time as *Mother Goose* at Stockport's Davenport Theatre. However, perhaps he had underestimated his overall health issues as he collapsed on stage during a performance in early 1995. It was yet another warning sign for this workaholic to take things easier, but it seemed he wanted to carry on regardless.

The exhaustive nature of pantomime was a strain for even the healthiest of performers, let alone one who was approaching 60 and not in the best of health. Though it wouldn't be the end of his panto career, he wisely took another break from performing the following Christmas.

Keeping John Inman away from his beloved public, however, was not easy. He accepted the offer of playing his hero Frank Randle in the 1995 TV special *Call Up the Stars*, appearing in character in a show that included Maureen Lipman, Ronnie Corbett, Harry Enfield, Su Pollard and many others. He was reaching 'national treasure' status with the British public but was steadily becoming more selective in his appearances.

In 1996, he was awarded a 'Gotcha!' on the *Noel Edmonds House Party*. The future host of *Deal or No Deal* supposedly set up John to speak with a delegate of American businessmen, with his popularity in the States the supposed hook.

Friend Peter Richards says the whole affair was a 'complete con' and that John was well aware of the supposed prank, which saw him press the wrong button and set off set thousands of pounds worth of fireworks 'by mistake'. 'You can watch the clip on YouTube,' says Richards. 'And you'll see John doesn't look very surprised at anything that happens!'

John agreed to return to panto in December 1997 to appear in *Snow White* at Southampton's Mayflower Theatre along with Lionel Blair and old friend Rula Lenska, who remembers reuniting with John and picking up their friendship with great fondness:

We had wonderful times together, not just working but as pals. I used to go to their house in Maida Vale every now and then and I played in panto twice with John. Once was in Southampton in 1997 and early 1998 and the second time was in Woking a year later. I was playing the wicked queen in *Snow White* and John was doing a piss-take of my very real wicked and nasty queen character and we had a wonderful time.

The two greatest icons I've done panto with are John and Les Dawson. They couldn't be further apart in types as people or the way they performed. With Les, you never knew what was happening – he'd do everything he could to make you giggle, corpse or whatever, whereas John, it was identical each time, very specific and never changed from day to day. He was very meticulous in his characterisation, in his make-up.

John was the star of the show and each production would last about a month over the Christmas period. We had adjoining dressing rooms. John gave me a cushion, with the words 'It ain't easy being queen' as a first-night present and I take that with me everywhere whenever I'm playing on stage. It always reminds me of him.

It was wonderful, and John was a very special man – very deep, very loyal, very warm, and I learned so much from him about performance. About the necessity of continuity, of always to be completely relied upon. We used to play jokes on each other on stage, but I always felt totally safe with John.

He was very generous as an actor – we used to work out little things together and he was incredibly warm when members of the public were waiting around for autographs and stuff like that. People differ – my ex-husband [Dennis Waterman] was not like that, but John was perfect – always acknowledging, always kind and always willing to sign things fans asked him to or whatever. At rehearsals, Ron was always there, in theatre Ron was always there, whether that was helping with make-up, cigarettes, drink or whatever – they were an amazingly strong, together couple.

The one thing that sticks out in my memory about John is that they were 'acceptable' gays for the time period. He was a private person, but very loving and warm and I had a lot of time for both of them – and that cushion goes everywhere with me.

In December 1997, John, Frank Thornton, Wendy Richard and Mollie Sugden we reunited for Trevor Bannister's *This Is Your Life*, with Michael Aspel presenting the Big Red Book. Bannister was reduced to tears, particularly by Mollie and John's appearance. John recounted a story of a toy shop episode of *Are You Being Served?* and the problems they had with the strict BBC security men – along with Trevor's sharp response that they were on their way to film *Play School*, to which they were immediately granted access!

John was back on stage in 1998 and certainly well enough to undertake a lengthy run in *Bedside Manners* with Linda Lusardi and Lionel Blair, playing to packed houses and rave reviews. He would follow that up with another successful stint as Henry in *My Fat Friend*. Feeling fitter and healthier than he had in a long while, he was diving back into projects that had been on hold while he recuperated. His long-time agent and friend Bill Roberton, it seems, was no longer managing John by this stage, with Phil Dale taking over.

John took an uncredited role in the worldwide box office smash *Shakespeare in Love*, as well as making a guest appearance in the TV movie *In the House With Cleopatra and Friends* – an eclectic special featuring the pop group Steps, footballers Ian Wright and Sol Campbell, Shane Ritchie and Wolf from *Gladiators*. He was still being true to his promise of several years earlier that he would pick and choose interesting projects and he was clearly respected by a younger generation of entertainers who could see a true professional and knew that when you hired John Inman, you got a complete performance with no half measures.

It had been something of a comeback year given his lighter workload over the mid-to-late 1990s and he rounded it off with a first appearance in the panto *Robin Hood* in Wolverhampton, alongside Zippy, George and Bungle from *Rainbow*, no less. A resurgent John Inman was hurtling his way towards the new millennium and showing no signs of hanging his panto frock up or, god forbid, retiring completely.

19

The Elder Statesman

John Inman was closing in on officially being a pensioner in 1999, which was his 65th year and his fifth decade in showbusiness. The fruits of his labours had made him a wealthy man and he had been with his long-term partner for twenty-five years. Although his years of heavy smoking had left him susceptible to chest infections and other related respiratory conditions, he was pacing himself and continuing to do only jobs that really appealed to him.

One example was when he appeared as Darth Sid in a hilarious *French and Saunders* send-up of the latest *Star Wars* movie. *Are You Being Served?* was still bringing in healthy repeat fees from around the world and it seemed there were new fans discovering Mr Humphries each and every year. He returned to the States again to tour and occasionally do TV specials, as Bill Young of KERA recounts:

John was extraordinarily nice. He would do whatever we wanted him to do, and we probably ran him ragged if truth be told. He presented the PBS special on Mollie Sugden, though for that we travelled over to England to film it with him. All his segments were shot at the Gore Hotel next to the Royal Albert Hall in London. Five of us came over for several days, we had a UK-based production coordinator and we filmed at the Gore penthouse suite.

It was going to be aired in December, but we filmed it in the summer and the poor guy was stood beside a roaring fireplace, dressed in winter clothing. At the end of the day, he took off his jacket and it was drenched in sweat, but he never once complained, and I think he enjoyed the recognition some fifteen-plus years after the show had ended. He never tired of meeting people, hearing their memories and sharing his own stories.

Whether he felt strong enough to take on a new lengthy run in a farce or was just content to enjoy a gentler life is open to conjecture, but he entered the year 2000 appearing in *Jack and the Beanstalk* at the Cliffs Pavilion in Southend.

Another interesting proposition was a movie cameo as Father Chinwag in the fantasy picture *The Mumbo Jumbo*, starring Brian Blessed, Joss Ackland and Sylvester McCoy. A bizarre, fantasy movie that is difficult to pigeonhole, Brian Blessed recalls:

I loved being in this film, there were many top leading actors involved. It was filmed in the forest regions of Germany, and parts of Surrey, England. The director Stephen Cookson became ill, and I took over directing the second part of the film.

We had mature actors like Joss Ackland, Nigel Davenport, Brian Murphy, Sylvester McCoy, and the delightful Melinda Messenger, and it made life easy for me. Not forgetting of course, the delightful John Inman, we virtually built the set together in Germany, as it was in a right mess. I owe John a debt of gratitude. It was the first time we had ever worked together. He was always so cheerful, unfortunately, we never worked together again – God knows why! We had so much in common. I suppose our ships sailed in different directions. I miss him dearly, what a gifted actor.

But despite the rest and occasional breaks, John's health was in decline and his breathing issues were not improving. In 2001 he had his worst episode yet and was rushed to St Mary's in Paddington yet again, this time spending three days in intensive care.

The damp, cold climate of Britain had led to suggestions from his doctor and close friends that he should spend more time in warmer climes, so he accepted the opportunity to return to Australia and, still in great demand, decided to tour with a stage version of the Australian *Are You Being Served?* playing in Brisbane and Perth.

One fan, writing on a Facebook fan site, gave an example of the type of consideration John Inman had for the people who came to watch him. Carol McAuley wrote on a 'Remembering John' Facebook page in 2019:

> My sister and I were in front row for this show in Brisbane, right in front of John and he kept turning his back to us because he was laughing so much. After the show he invited us into the bar and introduced us to all the cast. After drinks, he linked arms and walked us out of the theatre. Awesome memories.

Though details remain unconfirmed, it appears that John's mother, Mary, passed away in Blackpool in 2002 at the grand old age of 92.

John would also tour Australia with *Bedside Manners* in 2003 in what had become a second home for him and Ron, with the sunshine and clean air a huge benefit to his ailing health. Between 2000 and 2004 he played Aladdin in panto at Plymouth, Woking, Newcastle and Cardiff. He also accepted a small part in the BBC sketch show *Revolver*, by then in its second series. It featured former *Are You Being Served?* colleague Nicholas Smith, along with Honor Blackman, Roy Barraclough, Melvyn Hayes, Leslie Phillips and Gordon Kaye in a veteran line-up. It also provided Julie Goodyear, Bet Lynch in *Coronation Street*, with a chance to use her comic talents outside the cobbled streets of Weatherfield.

In her autobiography *Just Julie*, Goodyear gave a glimpse of the show's content when she wrote:

> In 2003 I did a comedy sketch programme for BBC Scotland called Revolver. I had a wonderful producer called Gary Chippington

and worked very closely with Melvyn Hayes, who's a fantastic comedy actor. It was filmed on location in Glasgow and I played eighteen different characters, which for an actress is like giving a kid a bag of toffees.

When you've played one character for as long as I did, to be given that kind of opportunity was heaven. And all eighteen were a long way from Bet – like a meths-drinking old tramp on the docks; an agoraphobic; a pathologist; Hettie at the National Trust; and Joyce who ran a brothel with a stair-lift! I thought Revolver was a quality show and really hoped that it would be recommissioned. But sadly that wasn't to be, as so often happens.

John would feature in all six episodes of the 2004 run, playing an eccentric antiques dealer who would reel off a dramatic, fictionalised story behind anything a customer wanted to purchase. The veteran cast's attempt at a quickfire sketch show were hampered by a script that was mildly amusing at best, at worst not that funny; think of a pensioners' version of *The Fast Show*.

John would also appear in the long-running BBC daytime drama *Doctors*, playing the character Teddy in an episode entitled 'Intolerance'. Filmed at Birmingham's Pebble Mill Studios, it was aired on 8 December 2004. The description in *Radio Times* was: 'A gay man appears to be the victim of prejudice'. From our interview in 2023, friend and former writer Tony Hare remembered: '*Doctors* would be the last thing he did on TV, and he again showed his versatility as an actor – something he was rarely given the opportunity of doing – and was again excellent, too, but he didn't look very well.'

However, old-school John Inman, who'd always told friends he would like to 'go' on stage, refused to listen to his body and pressed on with various engagements and appearances, although he was finding mobility more and more of a challenge. He may have been in his 70th year but he had begun preparations to appear in *Dick Whittington* at the Richmond Theatre to take him into 2005 – perhaps as one final farewell to panto, although the demands of performing were great for actors even half his age. However, he would never get the opportunity.

John was diagnosed with hepatitis A after reportedly eating con-taminated food and he was forced to withdraw, but the illness would push his fragile health to the precipice. Recounting a report of the time from the *Irish Examiner*, the website Chortle wrote:

Are You Being Served? star John Inman has been taken to hospital after contracting hepatitis A. The disease, which he contracted after eating contaminated food, forced him to cancel his opening night *appearance* in pantomime tonight.

'John has contracted hepatitis A through something he has eaten, and it has made him very weak,' said his manager Phil Dale.

'He is being nursed back to health and hopes to be out of hospi-tal on Saturday. He will need some time to recuperate but we hope to have him back in panto by December 20 at the latest.'

Inman, 68, was due to play Wanda the Cook in a production of *Dick Whittington* at the Richmond Theatre, south-west London.

He has also reportedly been suffering stress for the past three weeks since his London home was damaged by a fire.

Little information remains about the fire, the damage it caused or what indeed started it, but it was a home he adored, his safe place, and the experience was another trauma he could have well done without.

Doremy Vernon felt John had been pushing himself too hard for too long:

It's very tiring doing panto, with two performances per day and a matinee and two performances on a Saturday in a theatre filled with screaming children – it was such hard work. John was won-derful with children and it's a shame he had never considered adopting a child because he would have made a wonderful father, but things were different back then and his relationship with Ron was rocky at times.

John was a heavy smoker and as soon as he finished panto, he'd be smoking, and having a G&T or two and I think that eventually caught up with him. He was again taken to St Mary's Hospital in Paddington, which is a grim place at the best of times, and, of course, he had many visitors. Wendy Richard was there every day and Peter Richards was there continually, and he regularly held court by his hospital bed.

The debilitating effects of hepatitis meant John would never work again, and the knock-on effects of his illness, which attacks the liver, would make for a difficult last few years.

Perhaps sensing his time was limited, John entered a civil partnership with Ron Lynch in 2005, thanks to a new Labour ruling that allowed same-sex couples to be able to agree a civil union and attain legal rights should one of the partners pass away. It was perhaps the first high-profile and public civil partnership the UK had seen, and also John's first public admittance that Ron was his partner.

John and Ron were paving the way for many more couples to legally tie the knot in future years. The ceremony was low key and held at a Westminster Register Office on 23 December 2005. It was also John's way of protecting the love of his life, who could have been left with no legal right to his estate should he have died suddenly or become incapacitated.

He was eventually hospitalised and became weaker as the disease took hold. Yet John had still hoped to make a return to the stage, with *The Standard* claiming he had intended working again alongside his great friend Danny La Rue:

> Those who hoped that the star might make a final comeback were to be disappointed. A play entitled There's No Place Like a Home was written expressly for Inman and Danny La Rue by the impresario Paul Elliott.
>
> But La Rue, suffering from macular degeneration of the eyes, found himself unable to read the cue cards. And Inman, by that point, was too weak to walk across a stage.

In 2006, John also received some more distressing news when he was told of the bizarre death of former lover Kenneth Hendel. Christine Ozanne, who recalls when John and Ken had been a couple, said:

> There was not much TV in South Africa at that time, and Ken became popular, especially on radio, playing the lead in *Goodbye Mr Chips*, and the powers that be were very pleased with it.
>
> More work offers came along, and before long he had bought a house. He engaged a black maid who had a young son, who Ken also adopted. He came back to England only twice, and brought the boy with him.
>
> The story of Ken's death is quite dramatic. With ongoing back problems, he was being taken by ambulance for further treatment, placed in a wheelchair for the journey. The ambulance was involved in an altercation with another vehicle; the violence of the emergency stop caused the back doors to jolt open – apparently they had not been securely closed – causing the wheelchair to be flung out on to the road and causing Ken's death.

Although he had returned home for a period, it wasn't long before an incredibly poorly John Inman was readmitted to St Mary's for what would be the last time. Wendy Richard was a daily visitor as John became weaker and weaker.

Fay Hillier, learning of John's deterioration, recalls that a conversation with Ron made her realise the urgency of the situation:

> One of the reasons I went to see John was that Ronnie was exhausted, but didn't like to leave John. After I called up one day, he explained this to me, so I asked why didn't I come up and sit with John for the afternoon so Ronnie could stretch his legs and have a break? He was very pleased with that offer, so that's what I did. Most of the time, John was either dozing or asleep or barely conscious, but every now and then he'd come around and we'd remember something we'd worked on together or a shared memory.

After a time, I told John I was going to go because Ronnie was about to return and as I stood over him, he gently pulled my head down so he could say into my ear, 'Please take care of Ron for me.' I said that I would, as much as I could, and he added, 'Don't forget that I love you.' Those were the last words he said to me. I knew he loved me, and he knew I loved him, so I gave him a kiss, hugged and I left.

It was so touching because I didn't think he could even think that clearly at that point. He had what I understood to be chronic asthma and he certainly had problems breathing.

Mike Berry remembers the last time he saw his old friend in what were his final few days:

I went to see John on his deathbed, and it was sad because when I went in to see him, he sort of stared at me for a few seconds and then said, 'Goodness me, don't you look young?' I thought it was an odd thing to say, but he was really suffering at the time – you could see that.

John Inman passed away at 4 a.m. on 8 March 2007 aged 71, with his partner of more than thirty years, Ron Lynch, by his bedside. Wendy Richard had lost her closest friend and confidante, and as tributes flooded in, she was the first to pay tribute to a man she adored:

John's partner, Ron Lynch, phoned me at 6.30 a.m. to give me the sad news. I will always remember John in the good days. He was always immaculate and was one of the funniest and most inventive actors I have ever worked with.

Our time in the shop together were so much fun. We were all a great team. We did a summer season of *Are You Being Served?* in John's hometown of Blackpool where – in spite of it being one of the hottest summers ever – we played to packed houses, twice nightly, for four months. John was truly on the crest of the wave. He took Mr Humphries around the world.

The real Mr Grace, from Australia's Grace Brothers store, even gave John his own staff key! He was a typical Cancerian – a great homebody, a good cook, and an excellent host.

He never forgot his old friends, and birthdays were a joy at his house, where we would sit and reminisce about the old days. He was a brilliant pantomime dame – he used to study all the most popular ads at the time to work into his gags, such as the Honey Monster.

He was a very good straight actor as well as a comedic one. He will always be remembered for making us laugh, which is a good thing. He will be greatly missed not just by his friends, who loved him dearly, but also by his legion of fans on both sides of the Atlantic.

Peter Richards, friends with John for more than forty years, said:

He took his success in his stride, particularly in other countries like America, Australia, and Holland. It never fazed him, he didn't have anything to prove, and audiences loved him. I went out a lot with John socially and people would surround him – they just couldn't get enough of him. We'd go the theatre, restaurants or the pub and he was just so popular. I was very close to him because we gelled so well. John used to say to me, 'You'll outlive us all, Peter.'

John had suffered in his final years and 71 today seems a young age for him to have finally succumbed to his respiratory problems; although, combined with hepatitis A, the battle had simply become too much. He'd been struggling for more than a decade with ill health but had continued to work when he felt well enough. That love of performing and entertaining, as he'd said before, was a drug to him and not something he was ever going to give up easily.

With his affairs in order, his goodbyes said to those he loved the most and Ron by his side, he accepted it was his time. This most versatile, engaging and much-admired entertainer was, indeed, finally free.

As John succinctly put it several years earlier:

I've been to Australia five times, around the world three times and Mr Humphries was very popular everywhere. I was lucky to escape Mr Humphries and do many other things because of him.

For that, I'm very grateful to the mincing fool!

20

Dear John

John Inman was cremated at Golders Green Crematorium after a funeral on 23 March 2007. Wendy Richard, Trevor Bannister and Frank Thornton were in attendance, as were Barbara Windsor, Danny La Rue and Ron Lynch, as well as many other friends and celebrities such as Doremy Vernon, Miriam Margolyes and Christine Ozanne.

'It's a sad day but we'll give him a good send-off,' Barbara Windsor told waiting reporters prior to the service at Golders Green Crematorium. 'John Inman was without a doubt – and you'll see from the turnout – one of the loveliest, sweetest men in our business. I was very fortunate to have worked with him, and I knew him for over thirty years.'

Danny La Rue said he was, 'Sad, but doing OK,' adding, 'There are many happy memories for us, forty-four years we've known each other. This is for John.'

Christine Ozanne recalled, 'It was a very showbiz affair, with Danny La Rue giving the main tribute. The coffin was completely covered with flowers. Miriam and I went together to represent his time working on *Take a Letter Mr Jones*.'

Miriam Margolyes remembered only happy, warm times with her old friend of twenty-five years or so, adding:

He'd invite me around for meal at his home with Ron, or sometimes I'd invite John and Ron around for a meal at my house – not all the time, because I was out of the country a lot of the time. I lived in America for sixteen years, but I never lost touch with him, and I loved him.

We'd chat on the phone every now and then and he was just delightful and never changed at all over the years. Warm, open, and always keen to have a laugh and I think of him with complete affection and delight because he was adorable in every way imaginable. Ron was quiet and not anything to do with the business, but he was just a lovely, loyal man and he adored John, and he was his support and grounding, and they were lovely together.

I was 40 at the time I first met John and I'm 82 now and appeared on the cover of *Vogue* in 2023 naked. John would have loved that and would have laughed his head off!

Benidorm and *Loose Women* star Sherrie Hewson believes John could have done so much more had his health been better in later years. Having appeared on two series of *Inman and Friends*, she'd got to know him well enough to know he could have turned his hand to many other things. In my interview with Sherrie in 2023, she reflected:

I don't know why he never did any *Carry On* films earlier in his career. I think he would have been perfect for them. That said, he couldn't have played second fiddle to Kenneth Williams because they were both brilliant and both on a par with their standing and timing. John didn't do enough films in my opinion and maybe because *Are You Being Served?* was so successful, people couldn't see him doing anything else, which I thought was sad in some ways.

He'd wanted me to do a tour with him in *My Fat Friend*, but for one reason or another we just couldn't make it happen. I went to see many of his pantos but never managed to work in any of them with him.

I loved being with him and being around him and hearing his naughty stories. There were tensions in his relationship, but I didn't get involved or be part of any of that, but I'm just happy that I was part of his life.

Melanie Stace still regrets not having the opportunity to say good-bye to the man who played such a huge role in her becoming a successful actress:

> I went over to the US in 2006 as a host in a sort of Cirque du Soleil-type environment. But it was like a beautiful panto in many ways, and I always thought how John would have loved it so much. I told him about it and appearing in that helped me get my green card and I moved to New York permanently in 2009.
>
> I remember Ron calling me when I was in Seattle to tell me John was very poorly, and I'd always dreaded what might happen if somebody close to me fell ill while I was working so far away from home. When he told me, I was so upset and beside myself because I wasn't there to say goodbye and just tell him how much he meant me to me.

Bill Young of KERA PBS in Dallas wrote on John's passing:

> In 2003, John participated in our next special, *The Funny Ladies of British Comedy*, offering some amazing insights on his years of working with both Mollie Sugden and Wendy Richard taped at Mollie's house in Surrey, England.
>
> At the same time, we were fortunate to have John share a few more insights about years of working with Frank Thornton and Trevor Bannister on *Are You Being Served?* for our next special in 2004, *The Funny Blokes of British Comedy*. I'll never forget spending the day with John, Mollie, and Wendy, watching good friends reminisce about the days of working together on *Are You Being Served?* and *Are You Being Served, Again*. Even today, for me, that day adds a little extra to the laughter that all three continue to leave us with each week through their wonderful talent to make viewers smile. Cheers, John.

John left everything he owned – bar a small contribution to an enter-tainment charity – to his partner, Ron. It was four months before John's will was published on 31 July 2007, with *The Times* reporting, 'John Inman, of London W9, left estate valued at £2,800,250 net. He left £5,000 to The Entertainment Artistes' Benevolent Fund.'

Additionally, *The Independent* wrote, 'Inman stated in his will that the rest of his estate should be shared between his nieces Jacqueline Field and Deborah Inman, both of Blackpool if he was not survived for thirty days by Mr Lynch.'

It was an unusual caveat to add to his will, though he'd perhaps been genuinely concerned that, given Ron's fragile mental state as he struggled to come to terms with living his life without his partner of thirty-three years, it could even potentially result in Ron taking his own life. Should that have happened, he'd have wanted clarity for his brother Jeff's daughters, who many had expected to inherit the majority of his estate.

Property prices for Robert Close in Little Venice suggest that John and Ron's home could have been worth £1.4 million at the time of John's death – almost half the value of the estate he was leaving Ron. As Ron was seventeen years or so younger, if John had envisaged Ron living to the age of 80, could he have worked out that he was leaving his partner £50,000 per year to live on for the next thirty years?

Sadly, we'll never know, and, in truth, this was the will John wrote and signed – these were his final wishes. But there's no doubt-ing it caused considerable upset to certain people, as, inevitably, wills often do. Doremy Vernon said:

> I find it all a little sad. He gave £5,000 to charity and the rest to Ron, but Peter Richards was such a close friend, and he was just a dresser at Her Majesty's Theatre and couldn't even afford to go on holiday and I just find that awful that he didn't leave him anything.
>
> Actors can be very funny with wills, but I'm not sure how manipulative Ron was. I got along very well with Ron. I felt sorry for him. He was a very good-looking man when John first met him, and he was a Virgo so I knew exactly how to treat him. I

would always make a fuss of him and tell him I understood how difficult it must be to be the partner of somebody so famous and he thought the world of that.

Other people found Ron moody, and I can't imagine Frank Thornton being very nice to him when he was around the cast, though Mollie was. He was a chain-smoker and gradually became a heavy drinker towards the end of their time together, which I think became something of a strain.

They didn't go out very often, either – it was all about work for John, who used to say he wanted to die on stage. And, of course, he got very ill while still performing.

Christine Ozanne added:

John's will was such a surprise. He left £5,000 to Brinsworth House in Twickenham – a care home for elderly former entertainers that is supported by the Variety Artists Fund – but that's the only money he left to anyone other than Ron.

He had two nieces that he was very fond of, and I seriously think everyone thought he would leave them some of his estate, but they didn't get anything as far as I know, and I think they were very upset. It was very sad in that respect. Noelle Finch was in love with John – she was gay as well – and she was devoted to him and would go anywhere to see John or support him.

She'd drive him anywhere and do anything, but I think she was a little upset that he didn't remember her. The civil partnership meant that Ron could inherit his estate if necessary because without that and without a will, it would have gone to probate, and he might not have got a thing. Perhaps John had so many friends and people he cared about that he couldn't decide what to do and didn't want to leave anyone out, so left everyone out.

Within a year of John's death, Noelle Finch had also tragically passed away.

'John had been very fond of Noelle,' continued Ozanne:

She died a year after in 2008 aged 68. She had a good friend called Sally and they'd gone to Spain for a short break, but after being there a couple of days, Sally found her dead in bed one morning. She died in her sleep. It was so sad.

The fact is, Ron Lynch was John's husband and perhaps seeing his nieces and friends were all getting along well with their lives, he did what he had always intended to do – ensure the partner he loved dearly was comfortable for the rest of his life.

21

Being John Inman

In the immediate years after John Inman passed away, so too did other members of the original cast of *Are You Being Served?* – at a rapid rate.

Wendy Richard has been diagnosed with breast cancer in January 2008, just ten months on from the death of her beloved friend, and in February 2009 she lost her battle with the disease aged only 65. Just five months later, Mollie Sugden died of heart failure aged 86, and less than two years on, in July 2011, Trevor Bannister suffered a fatal heart attack while on his allotment, aged 76. Incredibly, writer David Croft died in his sleep two months after that.

Frank Thornton passed away in his sleep of natural causes on 16 March 2013, at the grand old age of 92, and when Nicholas Smith died aged 81 in December 2015, following complications from a head injury he'd suffered several weeks before, the entire original ensemble of *Are You Being Served?* were gone. Six fine actors plus a sitcom writing legend all gone in the space of eight years, although it's worth noting that many were of what is considered a 'good age' when they died.

It was perhaps poignant, given so many losses in a relatively short space of time, that on 28 August 2016 *Are You Being Served?* returned to the BBC with a one-off thirty-minute special to celebrate sixty years of sitcoms on the channel. It had been thirty-one years since the final episode of the original series and there was great anticipation to see how a completely new cast would perform with the backdrop of Grace Brothers and it would include the welcome return of Arthur Brough's character, Mr Grainger.

The *Radio Times*' preview read:

> The classic British sitcom returns for a celebratory special. Picking up where Jeremy Lloyd and David Croft's classic comedy left off, the show brings some of the nation's all-time favourite sitcom characters back to life with an all-star cast.
>
> It is 1988, and Young Mr Grace is determined to drag Grace Brothers into, well, 1988. But he has a problem on his hands. Mr Humphries, Captain Peacock, Mr Rumbold and Mrs Slocombe all seem to be stuck in another era. A new member of staff, Mr Conway, joins the team. But will he help shake things up, or will he just put a pussy among the pigeons?

On board were an impressive cast that included BAFTA-award-winning Jason Watkins (Mr Humphries), Sherrie Hewson (Mrs Slocombe), Roy Barraclough (Mr Grainger) and John Challis (Captain Peacock), with the production replicating the one-set, multi-camera recording in front of a live audience at the BBC studios at Media City in Salford, Greater Manchester.

Sherrie Hewson believed Watkins, who had found national acclaim for his superb portrayal of the eccentric landlord wrongly accused of murder in ITV's *The Lost Honour of Christopher Jeffries*, had the hardest task of all, replicating John Inman's portrayal of Mr Humphries. Hewson said:

> Jason is a wonderful actor and the hardest character anyone could play was Mr Humphries because that was John and whoever came in was going to feel that.
>
> I know Jason was well aware because it was such a difficult role to replicate. I knew Mollie quite well and knew her mannerisms and quirks and I thought John Challis was very good as well as

Captain Peacock, but Jason thought it was a daunting part because John was Mr Humphries.

For Watkins, the task of playing Mr Humphries was intriguing more than anything else – and too good to turn down.

The married father of five children was a little apprehensive of how, as a straight man, his portrayal would be received. He'd played the occasional camp role before in his career and in early 2024 he agreed to share his experiences on the *Are You Being Served?* tribute:

I would have love to have known what John was like off camera and out of the Mr Humphries role. It would have been really interesting because I imagine he wouldn't have been hugely dissimilar, but probably just turned the dial and enjoyed himself a little bit more.

I imagine they started to write for him very early on, even if that was consciously or otherwise, because of what he was giving to the show, and I guess he and the writers were informing each other of which way they thought the character should go to put him in situations that would deliver as much comedy as possible.

I just thought it would be fun. I'd see him as Mr Humphries when I was a kid – and we all loved the show, and all loved him – it was possibly a more innocent time and certainly it was for me because I was a lot younger.

All I remember about John and *Are You Being Served?* was a lot of joy and fun.

Now, things have become more complex and difficult and there are more lines that have been drawn and in many ways I think that process is always rattling around a bit in the background.

I was conscious about the producers deciding to have a straight man play a gay man as John's character is perceived generally, now. Was it a betrayal of gay men or gay people in general? For me, I just didn't feel it was at the time and I still don't feel that now.

I think it is OK for straight men to play gay people and I don't think that's a barrier at all, but that's a whole other conversation, of course.

In terms of his character, it was a joy to play John – and the whole idea of 'camp' you could almost say is a separate sexuality. One thing I spoke about at the time was how many gay men are actually camp, effeminate, emotionally strong, outgoing, and funny? That sort of flamboyance and extrovert camp gay is joyous, and I think most people will know someone like that whether at work or elsewhere. And whether they are like that all the time, I don't know, but that, to me, is separate to somebody who is gay.

As an actor, sexuality to me is the least interesting part of the person I am playing, and I felt that very much when I played Christopher Jeffries – and I still don't know Christopher's sexuality because I didn't find it interesting. What would knowing that unlock for me? I want to know how kind he is, how he treats his friends, his intellect, his compassion, and those are the things that interest me.

So in terms of the part, which is what I was doing – an actor playing a part – I was just capturing all that joy and I had no problem just doing an impersonation of him and celebrating John Inman and the show. What we did was nothing more than a nod and a celebration and though there was talk of it being a series afterwards, I wasn't so sure that would be a good idea anyway. It could only be a tribute.

But the level of skill from the actors in the original *Are You Being Served?*, and indeed the one-off special we did, was at such a high level. It came out of music hall, almost, and was informed by real incredible comic skill. The jokes are a bit old hat now, maybe, and there were some areas we wouldn't want to repeat or topics you'd be wary about structuring a joke around – and that's fine – but the skill in which it was made, performed, and produced is undeniable.

For my research, I just watched lots of old shows and did a little bit of reading around his career, such as the pantomimes, and after doing that for so many years he had that script for breakfast, really, didn't he? That was his meat and two veg, pardon the expression! That's what he excelled at and because it was a live studio audience, he could use them and play with them and you could imagine him taking over the floor and running the whole thing, couldn't you?

I know what we did was enjoyed. All I would say is that when we performed it, I do know it was the fastest-selling live show in Manchester that they'd ever had. It sold out immediately. There were maybe 400 people in the studio and there was such an enormous appetite for it. We created the set, had multi-camera set-ups. It was exactly the same as it was originally and when the cast came on to be introduced, I wish I'd been in character because I could imagine John would have taken over!

You could feel the sense of anticipation and as the music was played in the studio and you hear this theme tune you've known all your life pumping out and then suddenly you're there as John Inman arranging some gloves around a display and I could see my heart bouncing in my chest. It was so thrilling, nerve-wracking and brilliant all at the same time and the audience absolutely loved it.

Sherrie was wonderful, and she sort of embraced the whole event and she was so skilled. You could see the skill in those who came before us and she understood and performed it brilliantly because she had the funny bones that those comedy actors had during that period. Roy Barraclough had been there and done that, and for all that work he did with Les Dawson, he used all that skill as well.

The 2016 version of *Are You Being Served?* received mixed reviews and seemed to completely divide opinion in classic 'Marmite' style. Watkins gave his usual polished performance, Hewson did a fine job and Barraclough was impressive as Mr Grainger, but following in the footsteps of such a beloved sitcom was a near-impossible task and, as other sequels before it had shown, recreating a classic means it is open season for critics.

We'll include just a couple of reviews, first from *The Huffington Post*, for whom Ash Percival wrote:

It did manage to draw in five million viewers though, despite going up against ITV's big new period drama *Victoria*, starring Jenna Coleman, which attracted 5.4 million.

However, fans of the original series, which aired from 1972 to 1985 and starred the likes of Wendy Richard, John Inman, and Mollie Sugden, were less than impressed.

Many accused the BBC of ruining a classic, questioning the decision to bring it back, while others called it 'terrible' and 'unfunny'. The BBC's Sitcom Season continues with a prequel to *Keeping Up Appearances*, starring Kerry Howard as a young Hyacinth Bucket, which airs on Friday on BBC One.

The 2016 version of Grace Bothers was neither terrible nor unfunny, and to balance the critics' verdict, James Cornish, writing for the popular UK website Cultbox said:

The real standouts are Jason Watkins as Mr Humphries and Roy Barraclough as elderly Mr Grainger. Watkins in particular slots into his role very well and comes across as being able to put more of himself into the role than some of the other cast and isn't so much an imitation of his predecessor John Inman.

Despite its flaws, this is an undemanding piece of television that has a clear understanding and appreciation of the original (right down to using the original typeface and theme tune) and manages to pay tribute to it while maintaining some originality.

It's by no means a five-star laugh riot, but it does the job and feels like it could comfortably stretch to a six-episode run at some point.

22

Life Without John

Ron Lynch found life without John Inman initially unbearable and found some solace in alcohol. He had been devastated by the loss of a man he'd been alongside virtually every day for more than thirty-three years and, it seems fair to say, didn't really know how to move forward with his life. He had inherited John's fortune, but money seemed to mean little to him in the years after John's death, although he at least had the love and support of friends and family to ensure he wasn't cut adrift and forgotten about.

Along with his doting sister Linda, Su Pollard, Fay Hillier, Doremy Vernon and Peter Richards all rallied around Ron in the weeks and months after John's death with varying degrees of success. Su Pollard recalls:

> I loved Ron, we'd go to these awards ceremonies, or the Grand Order of Water Rats and we'd be conspiratorial and try and entertain ourselves and have a giggle and a chat.
>
> He adored John and John adored Ron and he was always with him. I don't think John could have operated without Ron to a certain degree, and vice versa – they were a very good couple, and Ron was very handsome.

It had taken a long time, but John had eventually decided he wasn't going to hide that anymore and was more willing to speak about his relationship, which I was very glad about.

After John died, Ron was sort of lost for a while, but I think he learned to cope with it and we carried on our friendship and would go to the theatre, or I'd visit him at Little Venice. It was marvellous to know both John and Ron. John enhanced your life.

It's not just work – you have to make the best memories you can so when you do go, people can recall some very happy times and that's how I remember John and I think Ron took some comfort from that.

Doremy Vernon added, 'Ron did nothing and didn't spend the money he'd inherited. I pleaded with him to go to places – he went for a day in Paris once and the odd trip here and there, but nothing of any real substance.'

Fay Hillier, making good on her promise to John that she would look after Ron as best she could, said:

Ron liked his drink, but I don't think he was an alcoholic – he was just a bit of a naughty boy, and he liked his booze a bit too much.

It was difficult being a sidekick to a star and I think he didn't have as much purpose in his life as he would have liked to have. John helped with that by giving him his diary to fill and letting him become his dresser because they were important roles to have.

He was a lot younger than John and I think he got tired of playing second fiddle sometimes and I know that occasionally he went out in the evening and stayed out all night.

John would call me and say, 'I don't know where Ronnie has gone,' and I'd offer to go and look for him, but he'd say things like, 'No it's OK, I'm going to pretend that he's in.'

I would go shopping with him or take him to Threshers or wherever he wanted to go and if I was having a lunch or dinner party, I'd always invite him over.

In January 2017, Ron Lynch was diagnosed with throat cancer, and his sister Linda would care for him until his death. Fay Hillier continued to visit Ron, who battled the disease for several months. She said:

> I went to Little Venice many times, even when Ronnie was so poorly. I don't know how he lived as long as he did because he was so ill and his sister Linda was looking after him,
>
> I'd continue to invite Ron to any gatherings I had, and he always came, even when he was dying himself. He always managed to get there.

Peter Richards believed Ron's reliance on alcohol got worse as time went by. 'Ron didn't do anything with his fortune other than go to the pub and drink,' he said:

> He went to seed after John's death. Sally, who was a neighbour from Maida Vale and friend of Noelle Finch, saw Ron in the pub all the time, either going in or staggering out. Ron had helped organise John's life quite well – maybe that's what he had needed.

On 15 June 2017, more than ten years after the passing of John Inman, Ron Lynch's six-month battle with cancer ended. He was 64 years old.

'John did drink a huge amount – though I never saw him drunk – but he was a heavy drinker,' says Christine Ozanne. 'Ron lived in the pub. He stayed in the same house in Little Venice, and he died there, too.'

Doremy Vernon added, 'Ron's estate went to his sister who was a lovely woman.'

Fay Hillier agreed:

> Linda was wonderful and such a nice person. She was around a lot and was there when John was ill as well, and she'd occasionally come out to various events, and she inherited Ronnie's estate, and I don't think John would have had any problem with that because he thought a lot of Linda and Ronnie's family.

The funeral was held at the West London Crematorium on Thursday, 29 June 2017. The service sheet gave the following information: 'Ronald William Lynch – 30th August 1952 to 15th June 2017 with donations to: St John's Hospice.' Peter Richards believes there were between forty and fifty people at the funeral, with family, some few friends and theatre contacts present.

The house at 33 Robert Close in Little Venice, Maida Vale, where John and Ron had enjoyed so many happy years, was finally sold and with it more than forty years of memories, laughter and the occasional heartache. Linda gave the sofa from Little Venice to Peter Richards – and he still has it to this day.

It seems the remaining family of John Inman and the remaining family of Ron Lynch do not communicate. Both John's niece Debra and Ron's sister Linda were offered the chance to be part of this biography but, perhaps understandably, declined the request for interviews.

On 19 February 2019, some twelve years after his death, some of John's memorabilia from *Are You Being Served?* was auctioned off in Thatcham, Berkshire, and was expected to raise around £2,000. The description of the items read:

In addition to his collection of *Are You Being Served?* memorabilia – which he accumulated over the course of the 13 years he played junior menswear assistant at Grace Brothers Department Store, Wilberforce Claybourne Humphries – fans of the late comedy actor will be able to bid on:

Inman's music and joke scripts.

Photos of him meeting the Queen and Queen Mother at the Royal Variety Show.

A variety of posters of his stage shows, including one which promoted the 1977 film adaptation of *Are You Being Served?*

Personal items, including a £1,000, 1950s gold Longines watch.

David Howe, specialist at Special Auction Services, added:

There is a whole range of memorabilia and props from John Inman's time in *Are You Being Served?* and many pantomimes. He also kept hold of posters, programmes and photos and it appears he went to great lengths to keep mementos of his illustrious career. Inman was one of the biggest TV stars of his time and this auction will allow his fans to get hold of items from his estate.

The auction raised £5,200, although it is not clear who sold the items or who bought them.

Of course, this is not the end of John Inman's story. In the pages that follow, we will examine the question that so many have an opinion on – was John a pioneer for gay people – or their biggest enemy?

23

John Inman: Pioneer or Harmful Stereotype?

John Inman, not wishing to offend his fanbase or upset his mother, would never publicly admit to being gay, as, of course, was his absolute right. He never played a role as a gay man until the episode of *Doctors* in 2004, and though he had lived with his partner for more than thirty-three years, he did not enter a civil partnership with Ron Lynch until he was 69 years old, so it's fair to say that it wasn't until the last years of his life that he felt comfortable enough to be open about his sexuality.

Some thirty years earlier, he had been confronted by protesters who believed he was hampering gay people's attempts to overcome discrimination with his portrayal of Mr Humphries. His friends say he was, at times, hounded by the publication *Gay News* to 'come out' as a gay man.

However, despite endless hints and innuendos, the character he played on the small screen never actually admitted being gay in any of the sixty-nine episodes. He didn't have to, and it was clever of David Croft and Jeremy Lloyd to leave that ambiguity in the show throughout its thirteen-year run.

Ultimately, however, Mr Humphries was just a fictional character and not a real person. Whether he was being himself or not, John Inman was an actor playing a part, with his dialogue written by others.

And as welcoming and friendly as he was to his legion of fans, John's private life was not public property and, as Mrs Slocombe might have said, he was unanimous in that.

Whether it was an open industry secret or not, in public he often appeared at high-profile events with a woman on his arm, whether Fay Hillier, Noelle Finch or any number of his many female friends. He'd privately told friends that the demographic of his fanbase was reason enough to keep his personal life out of the tabloids and it seems that, while his mother was alive, he didn't want to upset her in any way, though one would imagine she was well aware of everything and had been since he was a very young boy. It seems more likely he didn't want her to read anything negative about him, particularly his private affairs.

A delight to all who knew and loved him, he was not one to be browbeaten or forced to do anything he didn't want to do, and he had worked hard to get to a position of international fame. Doremy Vernon said:

> There was a lot of friction about John coming out as gay, I think because his mother was still alive.
>
> Then Sir Ian McKellen came out and told the world he was gay, and I remember John saying about him, 'What was that man's name who was an actor before he became gay?'
>
> I thought Sir Ian was a good actor, but now it's all about his sexuality and he pontificates and lords it about, and I think he may have put great pressure on John to come out as a gay man, though I don't know that to be a fact. As I understand, McKellen helped Michael Barrymore come out, but privately, when John was asked why he didn't as well, he'd respond, 'Why should I?' If he ever did, he wanted it to be his decision and his alone, not somebody else's.

The complaints by some protesters were that by portraying Mr Humphries the way he did, he was creating a stereotype of what gay people were like: light on their feet, incredibly camp with a mixture of flamboyance and waspish wit. And the fact is, there are gay people who are like that, but there is certainly a larger percentage who are not, and that, it seems, is where the two worlds collided.

Miriam Margolyes is one of our most cherished actors, as well as being one of the most well-known lesbians in the entertainment world. She believes it was completely wrong that activists hounded John at the height of his fame:

> He was a comic and he thought it was his job to make people laugh. He wasn't interested in being a political statement or standing up for gays.
>
> He wouldn't accept that heavy responsibility that some gay people always seem to want to put upon you. I know because I get sick of it. I don't speak for lesbians, and I don't feel it was fair on John to put pressure on him to take on the struggle.
>
> He would have certainly supported gay people and gay charities, but he wasn't a political man in any sense. They wanted him to be a different kind of person and he wasn't going to do that and it didn't sit easily with him. I know he was targeted by the more extreme factions of the gay rights movement who didn't like him portraying this sort of 'pansy' to the nation. People like Danny La Rue, Kenneth and John appealed to middle-aged women and grandmothers in their millions. John was a huge talent – he could sing, dance, and perform. He was loved as a colleague who was a golden man who was thoughtful and generous.

Melanie Stace saw John as a sort of father figure who took her under his wing, and she felt he quietly helped a wider acceptance of gay people by playing Mr Humphries:

> In his own way, he did forward the cause of gay people in this country, but not in an in your face, wham, bam thank you mam way.
>
> He had a great dignity, and he was the ultimate showbiz man, but there was nothing shallow about him or contrived. In my opinion, he did forward the cause, but he did it in his way and

that's how he wanted to do it. He was comfortable in his own skin and John was John and was just being himself.

Anyone who thinks he wasn't being true to himself is maybe being a little deluded because he didn't need to come out and say this, that or the other. Did Larry Grayson need to? My grandmother was comfortable with John, and she was 70 when she passed away in 1987. If somebody from that era could be comfortable and adore him the way she did, it showed John handled things in his own way and very successfully at that. He was doing great things long before anyone else and he still had so much to do. I was devastated by his loss. His was such an interesting life and a humble one at that. I loved that man.

The 1970s in Britain was an unforgiving place with racism, sexism and homophobia broadcast regularly via the television set up and down the land. To challenge attitudes was a risky roll of the dice for any artist, so while John Inman's character portrayal in *Are You Being Served?* may not have been subtle as such, representing a minority in such a popular way most certainly was.

Like it or not, he and a select few other performers were flagbearers for all who came after them and the general public not only accepted Mr Humphries and Larry Grayson's camp comedy, they embraced it with open arms. Some representation, surely, was better than none at all? Was it not true that John Inman and Larry Grayson were actually pushing the boundaries by making phrases like, 'I'm free', 'Shut that door!' and 'What a gay day?' incredibly popular in households up and down the land?

It is a debate that continues to this day. In March 2007, *The Guardian* wrote John's obituary:

Inman endeared himself to television audiences of millions as the show's character Mr Humphries but had to weather protestations of offence from militant gays who thought his comically limp-wristed gestures and mincing walk unfairly ridiculed homosexuals.

The character was one of the most arresting on the staff of Grace Brothers department store, which was created by the formidable comedy writers Jeremy Lloyd and David Croft.

'Inman became instantly recognisable wherever he went and had to respond with good humour when constantly asked in the street, 'Are you free?' – 'No, but I'm reasonable,' became one of his stock ripostes.

Some television critics described Inman and his Mr Humphries as two of the best friends of gay liberation on television. But the gratitude was not universal. In 1977, when *Are You Being Served?* had been running for four years, the Campaign for Homosexual Equality railed against Inman in Brighton, where he was appearing in a seaside show. They handed out leaflets arguing that most homosexuals did not behave like Mr Humphries; and they complained that Inman was contributing to television's distortion of the image of homosexuals.

Inman, not a strong swimmer in the fast-flowing river of controversy, argued that he was not campaigning in any way, merely trying to make people laugh. He kept it up (a typical Mr Humphries double entendre) in the series which lasted until 1985. There were compensations for him. *Are You Being Served?* lasted for sixty-nine episodes and made him famous not only in Britain but in America, where the series was sold.

Doremy Vernon points the finger at *Gay News* as one of John's biggest detractors, adding:

They were his biggest enemy and they were constantly trying to find out if he was gay or not, but he kept his sexuality to himself in that respect – everyone knew in the business of course. He once told me, 'Most of my fans are little old ladies and mums – I don't want to let them know I'm a poof.' And I didn't blame him at all.

But was the BBC part of the problem?

As recently as 2015, a feature on BBC newsreader John Nicolson in the *Daily Mail* suggested that the corporation was happy to bury its head in the sand and positively discourage any of its artists disclosing their sexuality. The article, by Matt Chorley, said:

The BBC officially claimed stars like Larry Grayson and John Inman were just 'waiting for the right woman to come along' because no-one could be openly gay, a former newsreader has revealed.

John Nicolson, who hosted *BBC Breakfast* and *Watchdog* before becoming an MP, said the press office staff at the corporation were 'aghast' when he revealed he had told the media he was gay.

He said that as recently as the year 2000, the BBC told him that 'no-one in any field had ever been openly gay'.

He was elected as East Dunbartonshire MP for the SNP in the general election in May. He came out in 1999, declaring: 'If my being open about my sexuality shows kids that people like Dale Winton aren't the only role models, then it must be quite good.'

Taking part in a debate in Parliament on diversity in public sector broadcasting, he revealed the shock in the BBC after they found out he had come out publicly.

He said: 'When I came out as gay when I was presenting *BBC Breakfast* on BBC 1, which I did for a number of years, I found that I was the first mainstream TV news presenter to do so.

'When I told the press office staff that I had given an interview to the *Daily Mail*, and that when asked about my home life I had been honest, they were aghast and told me that no BBC presenter had ever been openly gay before.'

'I said: "Perhaps in news nobody has been openly gay before, but what about other fields?"'

'They said that no one in any field had ever been openly gay. Larry Grayson and John Inman were, according to their BBC biographical notes, apparently just waiting for the right woman to come along.

'That was in the year 2000, and I am not sure that much has changed.'

As John Inman was so ingrained at the BBC, is it possible he was also briefed by his employers as to what was and wasn't acceptable of their stars?

In July 2007, acclaimed journalist Tim Teeman, now senior editor of the *Daily Beast* in New York, wrote in *The Times*:

> The 1970s are notable for the light entertainment shows that showcased the flamboyant flaming of John Inman, Dick Emery, and Larry Grayson.
>
> Many gay men of my generation view this period wearily – the limp wrists, ridiculous pink shirts, and innuendo-laden one-liners. But a good drag queen would have the same detractors roaring over their pints at their gay local on a Saturday night. The problem then, as now, is representation: when there is nothing else of gay life on TV, bar a mincing, desexualised clown, a gay kid growing up in the sticks would be forgiven for thinking he, too, was a freak. Although he minced and looked mighty odd, John Hurt's turn as Quentin Crisp in The Naked Civil Servant in 1975 was so radical – and remains so watching today – that you are left clapping and whooping in appreciation of 'the stately homo of England' who stood up for the right just to be different.

The Guardian's Alex Needham, now arts editor for the same newspaper, wrote a blog the day after John's death was announced and, like Teeman, felt Mr Humphries had done more harm than good. On 8 March 2007 he wrote:

> It will be interesting to see whether the *Are You Being Served?* star, who died early this morning, is reclaimed as a positive influence in gay culture. I hope not.
>
> About a year ago, Jon Savage sent me a CD he'd compiled of gay music from the early 50s to the mid-70s, when disco briefly blasted the closet door off and made gay culture almost mainstream. Not restricted by copyright laws (unlike the still-brilliant official version that came out last June), *Queer Noises* included such lairy

delights as the Rolling Stones' 'Cocksucker Blues', the Tornadoes' Joe Meek-produced 'Do You Come Here Often' and the New York Dolls' 'Trash'.

Towards the end was 'Are You Being Served, Sir?', a single released by John Inman that got to the dizzy heights of No. 39 in October 1975 – and the news that Inman had died at 4 a.m. this morning made me listen to it again.

Described by the late gay journalist and activist Kris Kirk as 'a comedy record that isn't remotely funny', 'Are You Being Served, Sir?' encapsulates everything that was loved and hated about John Inman's character Mr Humphries in the sitcom of the same name.

Starting with his catchphrase 'I'm free' the song sees Humphries demonstrating his sales technique in the menswear section of Grace Brothers, the department store where the show was set. *The Fast Show*'s 'suits you, sir' tailors had nothing on Mr Humphries: to a light jazz accompaniment, Inman delivers lines such as 'If you'd like some swimming trunks, we've got them pale or spotty/We've also got some see-through, that really tan your ...' then a voice, meant to be a lift attendant, announces 'beachwear!' 'Oh these are gay, I've got some round the back,' continues Inman. 'And if you want a bit of flash, then try a plastic mac!'

I have to say that *Are You Being Served?* – both the record and the series, which was huge when I was growing up, running from 1972 to 1985 – does make me laugh, although Mr Humphries undoubtedly perpetuated all the stereotypes of what gays (like me) are supposed to be. Mr Humphries is mincing and predatory, simultaneously pathetic – he lives with his mother – and a source of some fear (at the end of *Are You Being Served?* the song he's trapped the customer in the changing room which goes: 'I'm sorry that this fitting room is rather dark and chilly/Just try these on and mind that zip, in case you catch your ...' 'Sportswear!'). The writers Jeremy Lloyd and David Croft did their best to post-rationalise Humphries in the face of justifiable anger by gay activists, by saying that Humphries was never meant to be gay but just a mother's boy (as if). I seem to remember that Inman also cited the BBC as once ordering Croft to 'get rid of the poof', to which Croft replied 'if the poof goes, I go' – perhaps he was making the argument that Mr Humphries was at least improving gay visibility. Although was this the kind of representation the still-fledgling gay rights movement could have done without?

It's easy to trace the TV legacy of John Inman. Both he and the equally camp Larry Grayson, who presented the *Generation Game* around the same time, undoubtedly set a template for the gay man on telly, and to my mind it's only incredibly recently that we've arrived at gay TV presenters who can be funny without the punchline automatically being who they go to bed with – Simon Amstell is probably the best example. It'll be interesting to see whether his death and the many years since *Are You Being Served?* means that Inman is rehabilitated as a positive influence in gay culture and history. Though I'll still laugh at Mr Humphries (I've got a soft spot for Lloyd and Croft's comedies), I kind of hope not.

The author of this biography contacted Alex Needham to find out whether, after seventeen years, he still felt as strongly as he did at the time. He was happy to share his thoughts on his article:

I re-read my article and I do stand by it. It's complicated because one person – i.e. me – can't speak for all gay people. John Inman had a certain authenticity, but at the same time, he was emblematic of the stereotype that was around in the 1970s and that was the only representation that gay people got on TV at the time.

So it was John Inman and Larry Grayson who were huge light entertainers, and it wasn't their fault, but because there was very little representation of gay people in mainstream TV, they sort of became symbolic gay people and were figures of fun – not that that was bad in itself – but it's bad when that's the only representation there is.

Matthew Parris in *The Times* wrote a response to my blog saying he was always keen to see John Inman on TV, being himself and being quite outrageous, and I do take that point.

He was playing a character in sitcom so it wasn't that well-rounded in that sense, but what I do think is interesting given his reputation, is that sometimes people get rehabilitated and brought back into the fold where it will be claimed, 'actually, this person was important and this was a sort of landmark TV' but I don't think that's actually happened with John Inman, which to me sort of says people weren't happy with the way he represented gay people on TV. But at the same time, it wasn't his mission to carry gay rights forward – it's just how it ended up.

You can't really blame John Inman or writers David Croft and Jeremy Lloyd – I grew up loving those sitcoms – but they were of their time and, as we know, there were things that were on TV back then that are not fine now. People probably did get hurt at the time and perhaps said as much but weren't listened to back then.

Matthew Parris' response is another example of how John Inman divided opinion, perhaps like nobody before or since, right down the middle with little or no common ground. In his 2007 article, which may or may not have been a direct response to Needham's, Parris headlined his feature in *The Times*, 'I'm Free and it's all because of men like John Inman'. Wrote Parris:

> I raise a salute to that lifesaving human compromise, the open secret. I raise a salute to a band of comrades who, each in their different ways, were the keepers through a dark age of an open secret. My salute is to a dying breed: a breed whose ranks thinned again in the small hours of Thursday morning when John Inman passed away.
>
> Hail to them all: the ludicrous old queens; the drag artists; the pantomime homosexuals; the florid epicureans; the indulgent priests; the sensitive young men in tight trousers; and the wan aesthetes. And hail, too, to their quieter cousins: the discreetly confirmed bachelors, and 'he never married' brigade, the

don't-ask-don't-tell soldiers, and the dignified loners who just pre-ferred to stay single and wouldn't say why. Theirs – all of theirs – to protect and guard was a precious thing: the open secret.

For gay men in the 20th century the open secret was sometimes literally a lifesaver. It was the narrowest of territories: the half-acre that lies somewhere between absolute denial and outright confes-sion, between dishonesty and disgrace. This was a hard place to be in 1970, a narrow line to walk. If our oh-so-modern, who-gives-a-damn, 21st-century gays, of whom I am one, suppose that these men were not brave, that they were not trail-blazers, not part of the struggle, then we don't know the half of it.

And some of us, it seems, don't. Already I hear the cry – 'living a lie', 'set back the cause', 'self-oppression', 'an insulting stereotype' – from a gay lobby that has taken about five minutes to forget what a dark age England was for us, what light an Inman, a Kenneth Williams, a Danny La Rue or, from America, a Liberace brought into it, and how outrageous, how valiant, those people were.

About five minutes to forget, too, that the people who wanted these men taken off the stage, screen and wireless, were not the gay-rights campaigners but the bigots and guardians of conserva-tive morality. 'Sexual perversion', they said, wasn't entertainment: it was wicked and dangerous – and bad taste. The BBC, contem-plating making a series of *Are You Being Served?*, tried at first to insist that Mr Humphries was removed.

How fast we forget context. Always a bit of a giggle to their own era, the Inmans, La Rues and Williamses of the last century are now disowned by their newly brave inheritors: the lately and boldly Out. John Inman's breath had barely left his body before right-on spokesmen for that imaginary thing, the 'gay commu-nity', were berating the 'self-oppression' and 'stereotyping' of homosexuals that Inman's Mr Humphries helped to reinforce. His smutty innuendo, his jokes about fairies and handbags, his limp wrist, camp wit and simpering delivery are, they claim, everything we need to shed.

Yes, they are. Of course they are. They are now. But they weren't then. Then they were a light in the dark. Between the words, these men insinuated a wordless language of their own; they made a nonverbal statement, a shyly comical way of saying: 'This is who and what I am; this is my tribe – and, look, I'm famous and life is fun.' To anxious boys like me, who didn't even know a tribe existed, the lives and careers of these men showed we were not alone. You may say it was a pity it had to be done by double entendres. Yes it was a pity; but whether by single, double, or triple entendre, it was entendu. You could imply it, at last, and at least you could imply it, and nobody would lock you up. This was a huge step forward.

Remember before you sniff at the narrow caricature of a gay man conveyed by that old, camp guard, that these were the gays who didn't retreat into abusive relationships, dirty little broom-cupboard secrets, guilt, suicide, hatred, and shame – or surprisingly often the persecution of other gay men. They were the ones who didn't ruin women's lives with wretched sham marriages. Whatever the half-truths and timidities of their estate, they were in some deep way being true to themselves. In the manner in which they talked, dressed, and even walked, they were refusing to hide something. There is an inner honesty in this which is perhaps stronger than the honesty of signing up to a sexuality on a dotted line.

Their great achievement was to find a way, however comedic, to be themselves without becoming outcasts; and to show the world. It was desperately important to be able to do that 30 years ago.

Parris emotively concludes:

We gays can shed these stereotypes because we have outgrown them, because we have won the space and public respect to dispense with prison clothes and walk out of the virtual ghettos in which gay people used to bunch for mutual affirmation. We don't need to belong to a gang any more, to drink in the same pubs, congregate in the same occupations or dress or talk in ways designed to help us recognise each other, and help the outside world to guess without the unpleasantness of having to ask. We are no longer under siege. Everything can be talked about today.

But yesterday, when things weren't said, things had to be said without words. Men like Inman found the showbiz shorthand to do it. God rest their souls.

A stirring, emotional piece of writing by Parris, coming from a completely different angle than Needham, creating a fascinating debate that rages on – and certainly seemed to ignite so many different opinions back in 2007.

An article by Linda Rapp in the GLBT Archive said:

Like many other actors of his own and earlier times, when an acknowledgement of homosexuality could not only spell the end of a career but possibly make them a target of criminal prosecution, Inman remained closeted for most of his life. He generally deflected questions about his romantic interests by calling the stage his love. Sadly, as late as 1999, Inman felt the need to hide his sexual orientation, claiming that he had been in a romantic relationship with a woman – unnamed and unseen – for nearly thirty years, an assertion that was met with widespread incredulity. Inman came out publicly only when he and builder Ron Lynch, with whom he had been together for 33 years, were united as civil partners on December 23, 2005.

'Builder' Ron Lynch? Moving on swiftly …

In March 2023, *Sherlock* and *Dracula* writer Mark Gatiss, who found fame with the ground-breaking BBC comedy *The League of Gentlemen* – and who also became friends with fellow League member Jeremy Dyson after a long conversation about the forgotten John Inman sitcom *Odd Man Out*, wrote in *The Times* that he 'loved'

Larry Grayson 'as a kid', calling him – and figures like *Are You Being Served?* star John Inman – 'just part of a TV culture'. He went on:

> I didn't ever remember feeling 'pansy shame' or anything like that. I just thought they were funny.
>
> I grew up in a working-class town near Durham, my dad worked at the pit. Telling people you were gay in that situation wasn't easy. I came out to my friends when I was 15 and there were a few comments at school, but I was never bullied. The real problem for me in the Seventies and early Eighties was that I had no idea what to do about being gay.
>
> Apart from the occasional storyline in the drama series *Play for Today*, the only gay men on TV were John Inman and Larry Grayson. I played Larry in the ITV drama *Nolly* [about Noele Gordon, a star of the soap *Crossroads*] and understand why John and Larry were regarded as torchbearers. But some gay activists in the Seventies saw them as the enemy: screamingly gay, but at the same time a sort of neutered Saturday night camp.

Jason Watkins would appear in Gatiss' BBC Christmas ghost story *Lot No. 249* in December 2023, and he agrees with his friend that John Imman quietly broke down many barriers, without fuss and becoming a huge star in the process:

> John wasn't saying 'all gay people are like me' and I absolutely agree with Mark Gatiss because for the first time, you had a gay man at the centre of a hugely popular sitcom – maybe the most popular of the time – and you were laughing along with him and not at him.
>
> He was in control of the humour and wasn't the put upon victim of nasty homophobic characters making jokes about his sexuality – it was more that he was in control of it, and I think that went a long, long way.
>
> It was a family show with characters that would appeal to a family – a bit like a pantomime does – John is also the clown in

many ways, and it was almost straight out of a major farce. To have someone who was an openly gay, camp man in your living rooms and everyone enjoy it, goodness, I think that's a gift more than anything else.

24

There's Nothing Like a Dame

The argument that John Inman was a pioneer rather than a hindrance to so-called 'minority groups' doesn't end with Chapter 23 because he also played a dame in panto for more than forty years. Many believe he was the best. Was he, and those who came after, also opening the door to a whole new other world where men dressed – often outrageously – as women and were loved for doing so?

In December 2022, *The Spectator*'s Robert Gore Langton suggested drag artists and panto dames were also, in their own unique way, blazing a trail of sorts. He wrote, 'The panto dames may well have provided a safe space for guys who were theatrical and wanted to be performers, so there is a kind of bravery leaning into that – but the other side is that maybe many people thought that all gay people are like that?'

The pantomime dame is a whole new area of discussion, and is where this biography of John Inman will also conclude.

Broadcaster, actor and award-winning playwright Liam Rudden, who has spent more than forty years in the entertainment industry, met John – who had been a long-time comedy hero of his – in 1999. A lover of classic British sitcoms, and *Are You Being Served?* in particular, Rudden believes the likes of John Inman, Barry Howard, Stanley Baxter and Danny La Rue were all seamlessly raising awareness of and popularising drag long before the Lily Savages and RuPauls of this world.

Rudden says:

John was one of the country's greatest panto dames. Watching him, you could argue he was one of the first dames to bring some of the more glamorous elements of drag to the role. Drag wasn't something that panto dames used to do. Historically, they could be quite plain affairs.

Two of the great, but very different, panto dames of the 1970s were John and his *Are You Being Served?* co-star Trevor Bannister. Rudden continues:

In 1998, John was doing a play called *My Fat Friend* at the Edinburgh King's Theatre. I interviewed him on the phone for a preview in the local paper, the *Evening News*, and during our chat mentioned it would be nice to say 'hello' after the press preview. He said, 'Oh, yes, come and say hello.'

He was brilliant on stage. He did that thing some star turns would do years ago, whereby during the curtain call they would do a bit of stand-up. John did a twenty-minute old-school variety act with all the cast gathered around in the background.

When he came on to take his bow, he beamed, 'Oh I do like a warm hand on my entrance,' and I remember thinking at the time, 'Yes, those are the very lines Julian Clary is currently using for his walk-on ...' John had been saying them for years.

As planned, I met him briefly backstage after the show. I didn't really know what to expect even though I'd watched him all my life on *Are You Being Served?*, although I suppose I did have some general expectations from seeing him do interviews on the telly and having spoken to him on the phone.

Doing the job I have done for many years, I tend not to get starstruck, but when I met John, I went away feeling a bit melancholic as he seemed to be on his guard the whole time. The energy was strange too.

Having interviewed many, many actors over the years you quickly know how it's going to go. John's energy was unusual, there was an element of sadness about him but then they do say the clowns are often the ones hiding their troubles behind the laughs, the tears of a clown and all that. I left with that impression.

I'd taken a friend who was partially sighted with me as my +1 and John seemed reluctant to meet her too, until I explained her sight issues. He was absolutely brilliant with her.

Halfway through our chat I said to John that, 'Seeing you as Mr Humphries on telly showed me to it was alright to be "different".' That was the moment his attitude changed. He clearly didn't want to talk about anything like that.

I remember thinking, 'John, the whole world knows already!' Perhaps he'd kept his private life so private for so long, he didn't know how to take the compliment. That saddens me. He was perfectly polite, he did a picture with me, and we finished the chat, but I knew instantly that I needed to change the subject and go back to something safer.

That was my one and only meeting with him and I came away feeling he was a very complex man. I wish I'd had time to get to know him better as mutual friends tell me he was the most caring and generous friend when he got to know you.

I always liked John because was often given a hard time by elements of the gay press. It wasn't always like that. To begin with he was their darling until his type of camp gay man became a stereotype they didn't want.

Ironically, watching John on TV was one of the things that made me comfortable in my own skin and determined not to use sexuality as a defining label. He was just a really funny man that everybody loved and, like the Larry Graysons of this world, his campness meant people felt comfortable around him.

When you watched him, you laughed. Deconstructing his comedy as an adult, I believe entertainers such as John did far more good than bad, he changed perceptions and there are a lot of camp men out there.

If people who did feel threatened by gay people became unthreatened because John made them laugh, then perhaps they might question their homophobic tendencies the next time they met a person who was a bit camp in real life.

Characters like Mr Humphries broke down the barriers without knowing it. They started a conversation. TV has a huge role to play in society, educating through comedy – if you can make people laugh, they learn. Ignorance and fear comes from the unknown and people like John made that fear less. As importantly, seeing John on TV sent a positive message to many coming to terms with their sexuality at a time when their world was a very different place to today, that it was OK to be camp. They too felt safer and more confident by seeing people like John succeed on prime-time telly.

It's funny though, because apart from *Are You Being Served?* and *Grace and Favour*, I can't recall much else of his work on TV, and yet what he did do had such an impact on so many lives.

To conclude, John Inman left an indelible mark that is evident even today. A Google search sees his name mentioned in various articles – often with negative connotations – of how people acted or performed at certain times. 'He walked like John Inman', or 'his defence was as limp as John Inman's wrist' and many other, for want of a better description, disparaging remarks.

But he also opened doors for others that, with Larry Grayson firmly in mind, had been shut firmly before. In fact, 'I'm free' was voted the greatest comedy catchphrase of all time by comedy historian Robert Ross just a few years ago.

Most of all, he was loved by millions of people around the world, brought laughter and entertainment into the lives of all who knew him, and he always had time for his fans, never turning down a request for an autograph or a picture. He was kind, generous, thoughtful and caring and he was much loved by a legion of people who say it was their privilege to have called him a friend.

Above all else, that was his impact in a life less ordinary.

When asked – as he must have been many thousands of times – if he was free, he would respond, with a glint in his eye, 'No, but I'm reasonable.'

A gentle response from a gentle man.

Panto Appearances

1966–67 *Cinderella* – Gaumont Theatre, Doncaster
1969–70 *Cinderella* – The New Theatre, Oxford
1970–71 *Cinderella* – The Wimbledon Theatre
1972–73 *Cinderella* – The Bristol Hippodrome
1973–74 *Cinderella* – The Palace Theatre, Manchester
1976–77 *Mother Goose* – The Wimbledon Theatre
1977–78 *Mother Goose* – The Bristol Hippodrome
1978–79 *Mother Goose* – Theatre Royal, Nottingham
1979–80 *Mother Goose* – The New Theatre, Oxford
1980–81 *Mother Goose* – Davenport Theatre
1981–82 *Mother Goose* – Victoria Palace, London
1982–83 *Mother Goose* – Liverpool Empire
1983–84 *Mother Goose* – Alexandra, Birmingham
1984–85 *Mother Goose* – Churchill Theatre, Bromley
1985–86 *Aladdin* – Davenport Theatre, Stockport
1986–87 *Aladdin* – Grand Theatre, Wolverhampton
1987–88 *Babes in the Wood* – London Palladium
1988–89 *Goldilocks* – Grand Theatre, Swansea
1990–91 *Aladdin* – Churchill Theatre, Bromley
1991–92 *Mother Goose* – Theatre Royal, Brighton
1992–93 *Jack and the Beanstalk* – Bristol Hippodrome

1994–95 *Mother Goose* – Davenport Theatre, Stockport
1996–97 *Snow White* – Southampton Mayflower
1997–98 *Snow White* – New Victoria Theatre, Woking
1998–99 *Robin Hood* – Grand Theatre, Wolverhampton
1999–00 *Jack and the Beanstalk* – Cliffs Pavilion
2000–01 *Aladdin* – Theatre Royal, Plymouth
2001–02 *Aladdin* – New Victoria, Woking
2002–03 *Aladdin* – Theatre Royal, Newcastle
2003–04 *Aladdin* – New Theatre, Cardiff
2004–05 *Dick Whittington* – Richmond Theatre (forced to withdraw
   to due to ill health)

Index